Adieu

A Memoir of Holocaust Survival

Alfred J. Lakritz

BELMONTE PRESS

Calabasas, California

"Au milieu de l'hiver, j'ai découvert en moi un invincible été."
(In the middle of winter, I discovered in myself an invincible summer.)
— Albert Camus

The conscience of humanity is the foundation of all law.
We seek here a judgment expressing that conscience and
reaffirming under law the basic rights of man.
Attorney Ben Ferencz, Nuremberg Trials, 1947

Dedicated to

all my precious family members who did not survive

and

those whom I love who are with me now.

Table of Contents

CHAPTER 1

They Denied Me My Name

I was born Alfred Julius Weber.

I had the last name of Weber for one year. Then it was taken away from me. It was taken away before I could spell it, write it, or even say it. Imagine growing up with a name that is imposed upon you by a monstrous government that wishes to eradicate you simply because of your family's religious beliefs. That is how I grew up.

The German regime took that name away from my father, Simche Weber, too, in 1935; then it took his life. I grew up—in four countries, with three languages, little money, and only precious few moments with my father—with a name that was not actually mine. For years I did not know the facts of this theft or the circumstances of my father's death, but I eventually learned the truth behind both of those tragedies. I am writing it all down here and now so there is no doubt as to what happened to the name of Weber, to my family, and to me.

Weber is the name which was given to my grandfather Alter when he was born on January 10, 1865, presumably following other Weber ancestors before him. He was born in the Galicia region of the Austro-Hungarian Empire, now western Ukraine and southeastern Poland, in the town of Manasterczany-Stanislau. Since medieval times, Galicia, called Halych in Ukrainian, has been a place of conflict. Empires and kingdoms ebbed and flowed, claiming and then ceding their territory. In part because of these conflicts, Galicia was unusually diverse. It was not dominated by a single ethnicity, bloodline, or linguistic group. It was populated by Poles, Ruthenians—Ukrainians—plus Germans, Armenians, Slovaks, Roma ("gypsies"), and Jews. Its borders were porous and constantly changing. Its populations came and went in response to pogroms, wars, famines, and treaties.

Many of Europe's Jews found opportunities in this political tumult. Jews may not have necessarily been welcome in Galicia— the region was dominated by Catholic Poles and Greek Catholic Ukrainians—but they did not meet with fierce resistance either. As of 1910, 10 percent of Galicia's population was Jewish, including Hasidic Jews. In other places, such as the principalities and kingdoms that became France, Italy, and Spain, Jews were persecuted for centuries until the Enlightenment. They were forced into ghettos, not allowed to own land, not allowed to engage in professions. Throughout Europe, Christians often were not allowed to lend money or engage in banking, so some Jews went into those businesses. Other Jews became tailors and seamstresses, while some qualified as doctors and lawyers if they had the proper education or apprenticeship. Some were peddlers with carts, which they pushed through the streets; others became rag collectors, which enterprising Jews like my grandfather and father turned into a thriving business.

In Russia, the pogroms of the 1880s terrorized Jews. The czarist government attacked them in their homes, destroyed their villages, and even annihilated them by burning down their synagogues while they worshipped. Many German and Russian Jewish families that had the means and bravery made their way to Galicia, where, though it was one of the poorer provinces in eastern Europe, they enjoyed a degree of stability and freedom—at least for a while.

As was common during those days in Poland, Jews married religiously and not civilly. They followed the custom and practice of their people. The record of my grandfather's birth was verified along with those of other Jews in an Orthodox synagogue in Galicia.

My grandfather Alter Weber married Mirel Wiesner, a woman from a small town called Solotwina in what is now Ukraine. She was born August 4, 1874 and therefore was nine years younger than my grandfather. According to a family tree, the name Lakritz was among the last names of some of her relatives.

Alter and Mirel settled in Manasterczany-Stanislau and had all eight of their children there. One of those children, the next to last, was my father, Simche. He was born June 16, 1907. His siblings were Josef-Hermann (b.1894); Golda (b.1896); Necha (birthdate unknown); Chaja (b.1903); Hinda (b.1906); and the youngest was Schoje (b. 1908), otherwise known as Oskar. Oskar suffered from dwarfism.

My grandfather Alter was selected by his family to find a new home for everyone. His parents, siblings, and cousins had grown increasingly wary of the policies of the Austro-Hungarian Empire, which had controlled Galicia since 1867. Galicia's tolerance was eroding because of anti-Semitic actions by Russian Cossacks. The Russians captured young men and forced them into the army for a period of sixteen to eighteen years. Alter's family wanted to emigrate from Galicia in order to be protected from the pogroms and to keep the male children from forced military servitude.

The family considered Alter the most responsible, educated, and capable among them. At the age of forty-nine, he headed out in 1914 at the start of World War I, sparked by the assassination of Archduke Ferdinand, the heir to the Austro-Hungarian Empire. It would turn out to be a bloody four-year war that redrew the map of Europe.

Alter Weber was the extended family's most enterprising member and best hope for a better future. He intended to reach Norway or possibly Denmark. But on his way north from Galicia, he stopped in the northern German city of Kiel. He surveyed the town and saw that it was beautiful. It was located on the Baltic Sea, far different from landlocked Galicia, where generations were born, lived, and died without ever setting eyes on the open sea. Kiel was a university town. To my grandfather Alter, it seemed a peaceful, prosperous place to settle.

Kiel had a small Jewish community who had lived there for hundreds of years. They built a synagogue in 1910 on Goethe Street that was a beautiful structure, reflecting the organized, institutionalized nature of the congregation. The central wing of the synagogue was crowned by a huge dome, and the sanctuary could accommodate as many as 400 worshippers. The synagogue sponsored a religious school.

Instead of going to Norway, where he would have had to cross a border illegally into another country, my grandfather decided to stay in Kiel and see if he could make it. And he did.

Upon settling in Kiel, Alter sent for his wife and children. They left Galicia behind and, soon enough, Galicia itself was no more. Trampled over yet again in World War I, it ceased to exist in any meaningful sense. It was absorbed into Poland and Ukraine when the Polish state was restored after the war. World War I led to the redrawing of borders and countries that were once part of the Austro-Hungarian Empire and part of eastern Europe. The Peace of Riga, enacted on March 18, 1921, marked the official end of Galicia as a political entity, and the entire continent became an unstable place—ripe for despots to sell their inflammatory rhetoric. It would be only a matter of time before Hitler, Mussolini, and Franco would shake up the continent and cast a hostile eye on the Jews once again.

My grandfather acquired a piece of property in a commercial part of the city, just a few blocks from the harbor in the old town of Kiel on Grosser Kuhberg. You could call it a compound. It consisted of four buildings: an old building in which my family lived; another building where my grandmother and grandfather lived; and two additional buildings in the back of the compound for my grandfather's business.

In the period before World War II, Germany encouraged the collection and recycling of materials for purposes of conservation. The German economy was experiencing a severe depression brought about in part by the treaty reparations demanded by the victorious countries. My grandfather became a wholesaler of metal, clothing, wood, paper, and rags. People would sell him large quantities of cardboard and cloth by the bale and deliver it to his warehouse. In the warehouse they would be bundled into big boxes and containers, and he, in turn, would sell those gigantic piles or bales of cloth or paper, cardboard or whatnot, to another wholesaler or manufacturer who would recycle the materials. Many of the rags he collected were sold to the German government to turn into military uniforms. When he was old enough, my father, Simche, worked for my grandfather in his recycling business. He was a loving and devoted son and did what was expected of him as he followed in his father's footsteps. I don't know if any of his siblings worked in the business as well.

My grandfather gave jobs to other Ashkenazi and Hasidic Jews who had also emigrated from Galicia. Many of these Jews were, like him, Orthodox with long beards and black clothes. The men wore tallit prayer shawls beneath their coats and jackets that set them apart from the more assimilated Jews of Kiel, and certainly from the Gentiles. Their wives wore wigs and dresses with long skirts and long sleeves. Their clothing, their businesses, and their religious traditions made them stand out from the population at large.

My grandfather was a good and kind person. He did not take advantage of the people who worked for him; he gave them a living wage. His employees used to go around Kiel pushing carts and yelling, "This cart collects clothes!" and "This cart collects metal!" It was menial work, but what the peddlers earned kept them and their families from starving. My grandfather, being an immigrant, associated with other immigrant Jews who were Orthodox, unlike most of the local German-born Jews who followed less strict practices. Some of their traditions and practices created conflicts between these two groups. The immigrant Jews who followed Orthodoxy prayed every day in the morning and some in the afternoon; they remained close-knit with other members because the other Jews did not particularly care to befriend them or work with them. They were seen as outsiders, backward people whose main occupation in life was to read the Talmud and scriptures. It was decided—I do not know by what process—that they should establish their own synagogue.

My grandfather offered the loft of his warehouse building as a makeshift synagogue. That is where he conducted services. At the time that my family lived in Kiel there were about 600 Jews—immigrants and natives—who inhabited the city.

My father, Simche, followed his father's lead, conducting religious services in the warehouse. They had a precious Torah (which they might have brought from Galicia) and a shofar. Congregants generally brought their own prayer books. For my grandfather and grandmother, my father and mother, and their relatives, the Jewish religion was a font of joy and peace, of family, of tradition, of meaning to life, its purposes, and its rules.

Life evolved. My aunts and uncles who emigrated from Galicia found spouses. They married and had children. Some stayed in Kiel, while others moved elsewhere in Germany or abroad.

My mother was born Marjem Fass on December 27, 1904, in what is now Strzyżów, Poland, near my father's town in Galicia. Her family moved to Cologne, Germany, shortly after her birth. At some point she lived in Holland, but I know nothing about that period of her life and travels.

My mother and father met through a matchmaker—which was not unusual. My father traveled to Cologne from Kiel to meet this "suitable match" and was satisfied with my mother. Her family, like my father's, was extremely religious, which made her a compatible choice as a wife for my father. My father was three years younger than my mother, which was also not unusual at the time. In fact, some Jewish families thought that wives should be older than their husbands in order to bring out their maternal instinct and take care of their husbands.

They married in Cologne on August 11, 1933. Marjem's father paid a dowry equivalent to 100 Zuzim—the ancient Jewish currency—in silver coins, as well as various family treasures that amounted in worth to another 100 Zuzim. Simche brought Marjem back to Kiel, bidding farewell to her family. Her uncle—and father's brother—Max Fass, immigrated to the United States, settling in Oakland, California. One of her sisters moved to Antwerp, Belgium.

My mother and father were completely in love with each other and remained so throughout their marriage. A year or so after my parents married, my mother gave birth to me on June 1, 1934. I was named Alfred Julius Weber. My mother became pregnant again, and my sister Rosa was born on July 28, 1935. The baby lived for less than a day. She was too weak to survive. It was devastating to my mother to lose her daughter, but following the Jewish laws, my mother did not sit shiva for her infant—mourning the death of a baby was believed to be an impediment for becoming pregnant again quickly, which was seen as the remedy to this loss.

Rosa was buried in the Jewish cemetery in Kiel. She is the only member of my family buried in an official cemetery in Germany. Her death had a profound impact on my mother and made her sad on many occasions. But, soon thereafter, like a good Jewish wife, she gave birth to a second son, my brother, Herbert, on September 2, 1936. So we were a family of four, living off the money that my father and grandfather earned in their recycling business. They did what they could, and they made a decent living at it. Neither of them had a profession that they learned in school or in an apprenticeship, but they were very industrious and took advantage of the situation presented to them in Kiel.

As a family, I presume we were happy. But we were not born into happy times. Anti-Semitism had been rising throughout the former Austro-Hungarian Empire, causing many anxious moments in our family life.

In 1935 the Nazi government, under the chancellorship of Adolf Hitler, who had come into power in 1933, enacted the Nuremberg Race Laws. They were a set of 134 "pro-Aryan" regulations and decrees that targeted people whom the Nazis considered "degenerates" or otherwise antithetical to a pure Aryan state. These laws deprived Jews of citizenship in Germany, deprived them of their right to practice any profession, intermarry with Christians, or hire and retain Christians as employees. They then issued other directives and ordinances to further limit the rights of Jews. Jews were allowed to do only menial work. Jews were forbidden from riding public transportation or sitting on a park bench. Punishment was heaped one on top of the other. Rabbis were forced to clean the streets with toothbrushes, while Jewish stores were marked with the Star of David or shut down. Eventually Jews would have to wear yellow armbands with the Star of David.

Like many other Jews, my parents and grandparents prayed that Hitler would be removed from power and that reasonable politicians would lead the country back to prosperity. Of course, that was not the case. Hitler's attitude toward the Jews—blaming them for whatever economic ill had befallen the German people—

was a popular attitude, which grew only stronger the more the Jews were oppressed. It was like a cancer that spread through propaganda, and the German people were eager to adopt Hitler's slogans. My family, though, felt they had nothing to fear. After all, they were good citizens who minded their own business, and certainly had not the slightest means to threaten the new German state, but my family soon felt the weight of Nazi oppression bear down upon them. Hitler and his cadre of officials understood the value of propaganda and used it to convince anyone who would listen that they were Germany's saviors, and the Jews their worst enemies who needed to be dealt with in the harshest of ways.

In 1935 my family attempted to emigrate from Germany to the United States—more will be said about this later. What matters is that their emigration attempt failed, but its legacy lives on.

To process the exit visa, the Nazis demanded a copy of my father's birth certificate, as well as proof of his marriage to my mother. Presumably they wanted to ensure that the family, including me (my brother was not yet born), were all legitimately related and could be granted passage together. In reality, this was one of the many ways that the Nazis conducted a campaign to strip Jews of their legitimate family names as yet another form of humiliation and denigration.

In order to substitute for a birth certificate, the German government demanded that my grandfather Alter sign an affidavit attesting to the fact that Simche was his child. However, there was a sinister motive behind this affidavit. They really wanted Alter to testify that Simche was his *bastard* child. In other words, my grandfather had to acknowledge that he was not lawfully married to my grandmother. Therefore, they had seven children born out of wedlock, and my father was not entitled to share the last name of his father.

Whatever records existed that could prove that my grandfather and grandmother were lawfully married had been left behind in Galicia in the synagogue of the town in which they had lived. Moreover, in keeping with Jewish custom, their marriage was not a state or civil marriage. It was a religious marriage. It was a common practice in that time and place, but it did not count for much in the eyes of the Nazis.

The Germans instituted a criminal proceeding and a civil proceeding to settle this matter. In both proceedings, they declared that my parents were forbidden from using their married family name of Weber, and that they were, from that day forward, to go by the name of Lakritz. This affidavit, the ensuing orders of the civil court imposing a fine in the event of infraction, and the criminal court imposing the possibility of imprisonment all threatened my parents if they did not comply. So they did.

Lakritz is the maiden name of my maternal grandmother, who was born Mirel Lakritz. This is the name that my father had to adopt, and my mother did, too, lest she have a different name from her husband. My birth certificate changed, too, when I was about one-and-a-half years old. My brother, Herbert, was born with the name Lakritz in 1936. After all, it was easier to prove who is the mother who gave birth to a child than to prove who the father is. It could be any man in the community, so the Germans leaned into the names of the mothers and not the fathers. What an indignity that a father could not pass on his name to his children!

Years later, I began my pursuit to find proof of this travesty. In 1988, when I was fifty-four years old, I went to the German consulate in Los Angeles. I was asked about my history, and I told them that I had been born in Kiel, Germany, and that my grandfather had emigrated from Galicia to Kiel in 1914. The consulate helped me write a letter in German to the courts in Kiel requesting a copy of my birth certificate. I received a letter in which there was a copy of judgments ordering that my name be changed from Weber to Lakritz.

I am sure that my hands must have been shaking as I looked at these "legal documents" stripping me and my parents of our legitimate last name—Weber. And we were not the only family to be subjected to this travesty. There were many others who, with a stroke of a pen, had their legitimate family names stripped from them, but they could do nothing about it. At some point the Nazis even insisted that Jewish women take the name of Sarah and men take the name of Israel and that these names appear on all legal documents along with a "J" for *Juden*.

Lakritz means licorice. Every time I say it, it brings a bitter taste to my mouth.

* * *

Unbeknownst to me, the Germans reinstated our name after they had committed the most monstrous of crimes. After World War II, after Germany was defeated and some of its crimes were uncovered, they gathered all the recorded names of those people like my father and my grandfather whom they had arrested, deported, or killed into a collection of books referred to collectively as the *Gedenkbuch*.[1]

---

[1] The official name of this compilation is *Victims of the Persecution of Jews under the National Socialist Tyranny in Germany 1933–1945.*

The book was an enormous undertaking, with a weighty motivation. The Germans compiled it in repentance for the crimes they committed, in the belief that the families of the victims would want to know what happened to their loved ones. Survivors and descendants would not, it was hoped, have to rely upon stories, rumors, or alleged firsthand accounts such as "Yes, I saw your father taken to the gas chambers," or "I saw your uncle hanged in the yard at Auschwitz." The *Gedenkbuch* enshrines a reliable list of names and what happened to each person, including their manner of death.

I discovered the *Gedenkbuch* when I visited Yad Vashem Holocaust Museum in Jerusalem. I was on a trip as a member of the Valley Beth Shalom Synagogue in Encino, California with my wife, Judy, and my children.

I spoke with a gentleman at the museum's reception desk. I told him what I was searching for—the names of family members who had perished during the Holocaust. He asked me where I was born, and I told him Kiel, Germany.

"Don't bother filling out this form," he said. "I have the information concerning your family."

I don't know how he seemed so sure, but I waited for a few minutes. He came back with two heavy volumes. These books, he explained to me, were an accurate compilation by the West German government of the Jews who had been killed during the Holocaust.

I looked under the name of Lakritz. There were people by that name, but there was no Simche Lakritz or anyone with a first name of a family member. I then searched under the name of Weber, and there they were on page 1,550: Alter Weber, my grandfather, and Mirel Weber, my grandmother. Underneath that, I found the name of my father, Simche Lakritz Weber.

In death, they restored my father's name, the name they had stripped from him. You could have dropped an atomic bomb and I wouldn't have been more shocked.

Those books memorialize not only my paternal grandfather, grandmother, and my father. In total, thirty-one members of my father's family are recorded.

The information in the *Gedenkbuch* was based on Nazi records. It testifies to the care with which the Germans went to list the names of people who were deported, detained, massacred, and butchered. They recorded the information of their birth dates, the cities where they were born, where they were taken, the concentration camps where they were imprisoned, and some other words which may describe the means of their deaths. I would eventually learn of my father's fate many years after he died when I followed a paper trail to the Majdanek death camp in Lublin, Poland.

Seeing my family's names in that book gives me a certain measure of comfort. We cannot bring back the dead, and we cannot exorcise the hatred from the Nazis' hearts. But I like to think that thousands of other Jews of my generation and the generation that followed have also searched these books—just as they have visited Holocaust memorials and archives. Maybe they, too, rediscovered and even reclaimed family names that were stripped from them.

CHAPTER 2

Laundry Day

Sometimes, when I try to reach back to a time before the Holocaust, before the abduction and murder of my father, before the frantic escapes, before the breaking of glass, and before the dashed hopes, I wonder if, somewhere in the city of Kiel, there is living an old woman, the same age as me, in the company of her children and grandchildren and residing in a vastly different Germany than the one I knew, who, in her own moments of deep nostalgia, remembers a little boy of three or so who once took her hand and led her around the quays of the Kiel harbor, looking at the boats and prattling on as small children do, and wonders where he is and if he has lived a full life.

I don't remember her name. I don't know if I ever knew her name, nor do I know how we met. Eighty-five years later, I maintain those glimpses: her curly hair, the boats, and getting blissfully lost with her near the harbor or down one of the city's winding streets—my first, most fleeting friend.

Was she Jewish or Christian? Was she a resident or a visitor? Were her parents Nazis?

I don't know.

That is my clearest early memory, and it was a happy one. I cannot say it is my happiest memory, though. I have had many happy memories. But I will call it my purest memory. I lived that moment without any of the sorrows or fears that I was soon to accumulate.

She and I wandered the streets near our neighborhood with no idea of where we were going, or why, except that we were going on a happy adventure. Eventually people took notice of two small, unaccompanied children. Some very kind people asked us what we were doing wandering alone on the streets. We told them whatever we told them, and they said they would help us get home, and they did. These people were most likely Christians, but their religion did not matter. The fact is they guided us courteously, and with great success brought each of us to our respective homes, me back to my parents and grandparents who waited anxiously for my return—especially my mother, who always worried about me, a curious boy who sometimes didn't obey the rules of our household.

I lived in Kiel another year or so after that. I don't think I ever saw that girl again.

By then, Germany was already hurtling toward its horrific fate, with the German state and its ghastly cabal in the process of rewarding its worst people, turning good people bad, terrifying those who clung to their goodness, and demoralizing those who clutched at it only to feel it slip away. I want to believe that that girl remained good, even as she returned to the harbor and watched her brothers, cousins, and countrymen set out to sea under the swastika flag.

By then, I was long gone from Kiel. For decades, I never even considered whether I would ever return.

The city of Kiel sits on the southeastern side of the Jutland Peninsula, on the end of an eleven-mile inlet called the Kiel Fjord, which leads to Kiel Bay, which, in turn, opens to the Baltic Sea. It is one of the best harbors in the region. For most of its history, dating back to the thirteenth century, Kiel was part of Denmark. The Danes founded a university there in the seventeenth century. The territory was annexed by Prussia in 1866 and then became part of Germany in 1871. In the 1860s, Prussian King William I established a naval base and shipyard in Kiel, expanding the city's population dramatically from about 18,000 in 1864 to nearly 200,000 by 1910. By the time I was born, the city's population was about 270,000—a medium-sized city by German standards.

As in many European cities, Kiel expanded outward but maintained its medieval old city, full of crooked paths and densely packed buildings. This is where my family lived, at Grosser Kuhberg 37 in a three-story half-timber structure with a peaked roof that was probably 200 years old by the time we moved in. The name of the street as translated to English is "Large Cow Mountain." Perhaps at one time it was land for grazing cows. (Today it is the site of the city's sports arena; I do not know how or when my family's property was demolished.)

I don't think I ever considered myself German. Not just because Jews were marginalized citizens, but also because my grandparents settled there almost by luck, having escaped the chaos of Galicia. My grandparents could have just as easily settled in Copenhagen, Aarhus, Rotterdam, Hanover, Hamburg, Oslo, or any number of other cities across the European continent. Even so, Kiel served them well—at least as well as a city could serve a family of migrant Jews at that time—and I like to think that they served the city in kind.

If everything had gone according to plan, though, my time in Kiel would have been especially brief. I would have ended up far away from the Nazis and their war, traveling to the United States to join members of my mother's family. But the Nazis made sure that by reason of "technicalities," we were forbidden from leaving.

By the early 1930s, my parents and grandparents understood the evils that were welling up in Germany. They knew Jewish history well enough to know that yet another wave of persecution—of the sort that had terrorized and marginalized Jews for centuries—was rising again. When Hitler became chancellor in January 1933 and the Reischstag (Berlin's parliament building) burned a few weeks later, they knew that the Nazis' grip on power was total. (The fire in the Reichstag was blamed on the Communists whom the state said were planning a coup. It was further claimed that many Communists were Jewish, so the finger of guilt for the fire was pointed at the Jews.) It was easy to blame the Jews. They were scapegoated and resented for their successes and shunned for their failures.

In early 1936—without my knowing it—I experienced my first stroke of bad luck. (Many more would follow in my life, as would many strokes of good luck.)

During World War I, my great-uncle Max Fass had emigrated from Cologne, Germany, to the United States and settled in Oakland, California. He made quite a bit of money shortly after he arrived in Oakland but lost most of it in the stock market crash. He managed to get back on his feet. One of his daughters married into a successful family, and they all went into the scrap metal business.

I was two years old, and my mother was pregnant with my brother, Herbert. My mother wrote to her uncle Max about the conditions in Germany and told him that they wanted to immigrate to the United States. Max agreed to sponsor my mother, father, brother (who was on his way), and me. My grandparents did not want us to leave, but they gave us their blessing. They felt they were too old to make the trip. Besides, my grandfather was the leader of the Orthodox Jewish community, and if he left, what would happen to those who relied on him for religious leadership and the few Reichsmarks they earned as peddlers to support their families?

My father secured transportation to the United States in 1936 on the Holland America Line from the Port of Hamburg, which is not far from Kiel. It is south and west of Kiel, on the west side of the Jutland Peninsula, on the Elbe River. The Kiel Canal connects Kiel with the Elbe and, in turn, with Hamburg.

Everything was obtained, all the documentation, the tickets for the ship—everything, except one thing. That is always the rule: you are not done until you are *finally* done.

In order to leave Germany, we had to procure an exit visa.

My parents had resolved to leave everything behind: the apartment, the business, the synagogue, and the congregation. The congregation meant the world to my grandfather. His devoutness connected him to Kiel. He never would have left his faith behind, no matter the cost. And that is exactly what kept him in Kiel—that and his age. I think he believed that he and my grandmother were too old to start a new life. They would just hang on to what they had in Kiel and pray that Hitler and his minions would be defeated, that he and my grandmother would live out their days in relative comfort and safety.

My father traveled to Hamburg to make the final arrangements for our departure for the United States. It was a Saturday, and for that reason my father carried no cash in observance of the Jewish laws of the Sabbath. (Sometimes I have told this story a little differently. In another version, my mother and I are accompanying my father, and the three of us are ready to board the boat. I am not sure which version is the correct one.)

The clerk at the immigration office demanded that my father pay a fee for the exit visa, which was the final, obligatory document necessary for our departure to the United States. My father told him, "This day is a holy day, and I am forbidden from carrying money." He assured the functionary that he would come back the next day and bring the appropriate fee in order that his documents could be stamped as official. The functionary, instead, ordered my father, *"Raus matiaya Juden!"* ("Get out of here, you dirty Jew!") He single-handedly canceled our family's visa application. He could have done differently but looking at this Jewish man—Simche Lakritz—dressed in his traditional clothing with the fringe of his tallit peeking out from under his black coat, he railed against him, thereby shutting the door on our passage to safety.

A letter dated March 20, 1936, addressed to my great-uncle Max Fass from the Holland American Line informed him that the passengers whom he had sponsored had not received their required visas. They were, therefore, not allowed to board the ship, as Max had arranged. There was nothing my great-uncle could do. He was in the United States. The shipping line needed to see a legitimate visa. We were stuck.

Were there laws at the time forbidding Jews to leave? I think not. The policy of Germany was to encourage them to leave—but not before they took their pound of flesh and paid what was known as a "flight tax." That tax was calculated based upon the assets of a family that were kept in records available to the Nazis. Usually, the records were stored in synagogues. Where they were kept in Kiel is not known to me. The functionary clearly felt like punishing us, denying us the opportunity to leave for the United States.

It seemed that on the particular day that my father went before the functionary in Hamburg, he was unlucky enough to stand before someone who considered money more important than ridding Germany of this particular dirty Jew, Simche LaKritz, neé Weber, and his wife, son, and soon-to-be-born baby. Maybe he knew that there were other plans to take care of the Jews—more sinister than anyone could have imagined. But for the moment we had to forfeit our tickets and stay trapped in Kiel, wondering what would happen next to the immigrant Jews of the city and to our family.

* * *

Instead of moving to the safe harbor of Oakland, California, with the Fass family, I grew from infant to toddler to child in Kiel. My father ran the rag and recycling business as best he could with my grandfather, and he made a comfortable life for us. I, of course, knew nothing of Hitler or Nazis or anti-Semitism at the time. I can only imagine, though, the anxiety my parents must have felt waking up every morning in a country whose hatred for them grew, each day, like a prison wall rising brick by brick.

I lived in many places from my birth to age sixteen, and I associate each of those old memories with different places. The memories are only glimpses. I see them as if through a small window, a window that was to be irreparably shattered the night of November 9, 1938.

I had pleasant times before then.

There was a crispness, a coldness, and a freshness to the air in Kiel. My home was only a few blocks from the wharf, beyond which was the open Baltic Sea. I remember watching the boats and hearing maritime sounds: clangs, and horns, and shouts of sailors, speaking of the sea.

I remember my grandfather's property on Grosser Kuhberg, to some degree. (I have since looked at the location on historical and modern maps, which refreshed my memory a bit.) We lived on the second story of a building, and our apartment faced a major boulevard. The Weidmanns, my mother's cousins, lived beneath us on the first floor. They might have emigrated from Cologne soon after my grandfather settled his family in Kiel.

Then there was a driveway, and down that driveway was the building where my grandfather and grandmother lived. To the left of that, in the back, were warehouses where the family business was located and where my grandfather had his makeshift synagogue. There was storage for bales of cloth collected by the peddlers. I remember playing on the bales, bounding from one to another with my Weidmann cousins and other youngsters in our family, playing versions of tag.

A tapestry hung on the wall of our living room. The main figure on that tapestry was a deer. The Austrians and Germans love hunting scenes with bugles, dogs, and quarry. I always thought the deer was following me with his eyes as I moved in the room in front of him. That was really strange, and it frightened me.

One evening my parents had to leave us for a family gathering or religious service—something where they were both expected to be present. They left me responsible for myself and my younger brother, Herbert. I was three, or maybe approaching four. My parents expected that I would be responsible enough for the hour or two that they would be absent.

I became afraid because my parents were not there. I was afraid that there might be demons or something; everything frightened me—sounds, darkness, and of course, blood. I was a very anxious child, which might have been the result of having parents who were worried every day of what the government might do to them. Their anxiety poured over onto me, even if they tried to hide their legitimate concerns.

I turned on all the lights in our apartment. Not hearing anything, I went to my parents' bedroom with my brother in tow. We started jumping on the bed. On one of those jumps, I fell and hit the corner of the night table. I bled, and a huge bruise developed immediately. I don't remember what I did. I must have sat there and cried. Herbert probably cried too.

When my parents came home, you can imagine how they felt. I had hit my forehead, so they had to take me to a doctor at the hospital to stitch it up. To this day, I still have a little scar.

I remember a Passover seder dinner. My father was dressed all in white, with a white kippah and a white gown, and we ate dinner on the floor, reclining. This is the first of many seders that I remember. We still observe Passover every year, and it is a holiday when I often reflect on those times with relatives that seemed happy to me—reading from the Haggadah; reciting the four questions (*Ma Nishtana*); singing songs such as "Dayenu" ("It would have been enough") before and after the meal; looking for the matzoh that my father hid for the children to find and receive a reward; and inviting Elijah to return with the messiah.

I also remember something that really, truly frightened me. One day my mother was hanging drapes she had made for a window in our living room, and she fell off the ladder, or perhaps it was a chair. I don't think I saw her fall, but I know what I did see. I saw people coming to take my mother away in an ambulance. I could not understand that. I only understood that they were taking my mother away. I cried, and I still cry. I was absolutely bereft.

I think often of the differences between personal pain and general pain. My mother's accident, minor as it was, struck me personally. She was, in a way, bigger to me than the entire rest of the world. And yet, the rest of the world was soon to face an overwhelming trauma. Millions of people would die. Millions more would suffer injury and bodily pain. And for each of them, sons, daughters, mothers, fathers, and siblings would amplify the trauma, feeling it in their bones, suffering, perhaps, more acutely, and for far longer—decades, in fact—than did the direct victims themselves.

But when I was four years old, the mere thought of being apart from my mother was the most traumatic thing I could imagine. I wasn't yet aware of the family separations that would take place at the hands of the Nazis. My fear was purely emotional, based on the indelible bond between a mother and child. Our family, and our family compound, was an island of safety in what was becoming a city full of dangers.

I saw Nazis themselves. One day in 1937 or 1938, military maneuvers took place in front of our apartment. My father and I watched from our crouched positions behind the drapes of our window. I learned that I had to be careful not to show ourselves to the Gestapo.

"I want to look," I said. I wanted to see these men and what they were doing, and my father said, "Okay, you can look, but stay on the floor, and only look just to the corner of the drapes." I did so, and there were all these men in uniform marching and a band playing, and I had never seen such a thing. I don't know if they were on training maneuvers or were there to warn us of what was to follow—that people were to be rounded up and taken away.

One day I visited my grandfather and grandmother, who lived next door. When I approached the house, my grandfather sat in the front room dressed in the style of a Hasidic Jew with his long pepper-gray beard and a hat. He looked at me and started to tease me about my suspenders. I did not like that he was making fun of me. I thought my suspenders were very nice. After all, my mother had chosen them for me, and I thought that whatever my mother did was right and perfect. To me, my mother was an angel who could do no wrong. When I was next to her, I felt safe, and when I was separated from her, I was scared.

That was the first experience I had of being ridiculed. I carry not only the emotional discomfort of that memory but also a sense of bewilderment. Over the coming years, I was to confront some of the ugliest offenses in human existence. Teasing me about suspenders seems petty and unnecessary. But maybe that's what grandfathers do. Maybe it was one way he had to distract himself from the world. Maybe he thought he was just making a joke, but it hurt me deeply. Or maybe he thought he was toughening me up—that maybe I was a mama's boy and if I was to make it in the world, I shouldn't be affected by teasing. I should just laugh it off. But I wasn't that kind of a child. I was sensitive and fearful.

* * *

Kristallnacht, the Night of Broken Glass, took place on November 9-10, 1938—more than two years after we had planned to leave Germany for the United States. The Nazis came and burned the prayer books, shawls, and anything else of a religious nature in my grandfather's synagogue, which was housed in the warehouse. The Gestapo set them on fire in the street in front of the compound and made a show of what they were doing to us. Throughout the city of Kiel, they burned down stores owned by Jews, burned homes, burned synagogues, and attacked people to intimidate the Jews. Nazis marched through the streets; people rioted, and nothing was the same from then on. We did not know who was our enemy and who was our friend. The spark that set off this rampage against the Jews began in Paris, where a Polish Jew killed a German soldier. The Nazis saw this as an excuse for two days of terror and punishment against Jewish communities in Germany and elsewhere.

Many years later I learned that the soldiers and hoodlums who terrorized Germany's Jews that night were careful not to destroy places where official records were stored. They wanted to refer to those records to officially identify Jews, appropriate their property, and ultimately round them up and send them away. Many of these records included documents listing the assets of the Jews—what properties they owned, where their bank accounts were kept, what equipment and machinery they might have owned, and so forth—so that the Nazis could determine the amount of the flight tax to be pried out of their hands and take whatever belonged to them.

Kristallnacht was not a spontaneous conflagration. It was a carefully planned operation relying on the general population to help carry out the destruction. Many Germans willingly participated in the carnage to get rid of the "vermin" and to steal their belongings for themselves. Some of this stolen chattel was used to buy the loyalty of Germans who might have been on the fence about whether to support the Nazi Party or resist them. By 1936, probably over 90 percent of the German people were, in some degree, supporters of the Nazi regime.

After Kristallnacht, the Nazis intensified pressure on the Jews to leave. The Nazis wanted them to go to Poland, where they assumed they would be among their own kind. Apparently, Poland had been accepting refugees dumped on the border between Poland and Germany at the Oder River where the trains crossed.

Out of the blue, two soldiers came to arrest us sometime after Kristallnacht. They banged on our apartment door and demanded entry. They had rifles with bayonets. I had never seen weapons like that, except with the soldiers who had paraded in front of our apartment.

One of the soldiers stood on the landing on the second floor of our apartment building. I looked at him and his gun and his uniform. He was quiet. He didn't say anything to me that I remember. Maybe he was nice to me; I don't know.

They demanded that we leave our home, pack up our belongings, and grab whatever we needed for wherever they were going to take us. I think they shouted that we were going to be transported across the border to Poland—this was where the Nazis planned on dumping the Jews. My parents had no foreknowledge of any such order. They were not prepared, but the same thing was happening to other Jews in the city of Kiel and elsewhere. I don't know why we were targeted at this point. Was it because we had money? Was it because we had a business that they could appropriate? Was it because we had tried to leave two years before unsuccessfully? Or was it that we were unlucky?

I am sure that my mother advised them that my father was working for his father in his business that was next door to our apartment, and he would come right along. He came, and he likewise was then placed under arrest along with my mother.

It was laundry day, and our clothes were on a clothesline on the roof. My mother explained this to the soldiers and asked them to allow her to go up and collect the wet laundry. The soldiers agreed, but one of them accompanied her to the roof so that she would not try to run away. She put our clothes into two bags, and we were allowed to take just those two bags.

We were arrested and dragged to some form of detention area with other Jews. Then we were taken to the railroad station and put on a train bound for the German-Polish border.

Devout Jewish men on the train were davening and wailing, frightened within an inch of their lives, not knowing what lay in store. I was with my father; my brother, Herbert, was with my mother. I had never seen men cry. I cried, of course. And I saw other children cry. But never men. The train made stops along the route. I remember people at some stops gave us chocolates. I also remember getting off the train with my mother so I could "make water," and for the first time I saw my mother also making water.

That might have been when I realized the anatomical differences between men and women.

The train arrived at the Polish border, on the Oder River, after many hours. By some twist of fate, Poland had closed its border that day and said "no more" to the Germans: no more Jews, no more deportations. Our train was ordered to return to Kiel.

Had we crossed that border, we would have settled in the Jewish quarter of a Polish city or maybe a small town. We would have met people with similar backgrounds, bound by a common history, culture, and faith. We'd have communicated in Yiddish; it might have become my primary language. I'd have gone to school, made friends, gone to synagogue, shared the love of my family. And I surely would have died within a few years once the Nazis put their killing machines into full operation. Escaping from Poland all the way to the relative safety of Western Europe would have been impossible. We would have been forced into a ghetto, then taken to a labor camp, and then to a concentration camp. My death would have been one minuscule contribution to "solving" what the Nazis eventually termed "the Jewish Problem."

From that day forward, when we returned from the border, I know that my mother and father realized this was the final straw and that they had to leave for their children and for their own sake. Soon enough, Germany invaded Poland to create *Lebensraum*—the racist notion that the German race was entitled to more "living space"—and put an end to the Poles dictating to the Germans what they could and could not do.

That is when my parents arranged for us to be smuggled out of Germany into Belgium. I'm sure I never said goodbye to the girl with the curly hair who held my hand as we walked along the quays of Kiel. I don't know if she lived only a few more years or if she is alive in Kiel today, listening to the sounds of the harbor and remembering the little boy who accompanied her on her wanderings, or if she and her family also ran for their lives.

My mother's father, Moses Willner.

My mother, Marjem Willner, with her mother Rachel
and her brother, Michael, in Galicia/Poland.

My mother as a young girl. This photograph may have
been taken in Cologne, Germany.

My parents Marjem Willner and Simche Weber shortly before their marriage.

My parents on their wedding day, August 11, 1933.

Panorama of Kiel, early 20th century.

My mother's relatives visiting Kiel.
(L-R) My Aunt Ida and my Uncle Michael Fass and my mother's parents,
and unidentified relatives (perhaps Max Fass and his wife).

CHAPTER 3

Refusing to Learn My ABCs

My father and mother investigated how we could escape. Desperate to get out of Germany and as far as possible from the Nazis, my parents came up with a plan. Time was of the essence.

Within Europe, Jews escaped to the countries of the United Kingdom, the Netherlands, Belgium, France, and Poland in the greatest numbers, at over 30,000 each. Traveling even farther, some 55,000 Jews fled to Palestine (before the State of Israel was founded), 45,000 went to Argentina, 26,000 to South Africa, and 20,000 as far away as Shanghai, China, by the time the war was over. The greatest number by far—over 100,000—went to the United States. But tens of thousands more remained in Germany, and millions were in surrounding countries that came under Nazi control as borders closed and even friendly nations were unwilling to assume responsibility for immigrants seeking asylum.

I don't know what distinguished those families who fled from those who remained. In some cases, it was surely money—they did not have the funds to pay for the smugglers and bribes. Some might have been optimistic, thinking that the tide would turn and that Hitler would be defeated and life would return to normal, even after the Kristallnacht rampage against the Jews. Others might have been held back by aged relatives, or they might have lived too far from transportation routes or borders to imagine the journey to (supposedly) safe countries like Belgium, France, and England. And still others were deluded into thinking that they were "true Germans" who had served in the First World War, had earned medals of honor, had accepted their military loss with grace, and who owned land and status that would somehow shield them from harm.

There were many Jews who had at one time been treated like royalty in the Austro-Hungarian Empire, serving the crown. And there were Jews who had amassed enormous wealth along Vienna's Ringstrasse, with villas that rivaled the homes of European monarchs. In time, these families would not escape the wrath of Hitler. He and his minions would appropriate their treasures, raid their banks, and make sure they left their countries with nothing but the clothes on their backs.

During the year that my parents negotiated their own escape, life in Kiel became untenable. Jews were forced to clean the streets with toothbrushes; they weren't allowed to sit on benches in the parks; they were denied the right to work; their shops were taken over by non-Jews; many families were taken away. The Nazis confiscated bank accounts and stole treasures that had been amassed by wealthy Jews. The Nazis redistributed some of these possessions to "good citizens" as a means of buying their loyalty to the party. Jewish shops were either shuttered or had *"Juden"* written on the door so that people wouldn't come in; children of school age were told to stay home. Life was becoming a living hell for Jews, and it would be only a matter of time before something worse would happen to my family. Postwar records indicate that a total of 586 Jews left Kiel during the Nazi era. Of those who remained, eighty-five were deportees and twelve committed suicide. After the war, eleven Jews returned to Kiel.

Our escape took place one evening in August 1939, not quite a year after Kristallnacht, and a month before the start of World War II with the German invasion of Poland and the declaration of war by England and France. We were smuggled by paid persons into Belgium. We must have traveled by train quite a ways to the border of Germany and Belgium, over 480 kilometers from Kiel. I had to walk along an area where there was barbed wire. I must have been very much aware that we were in danger of capture. I am sure that our paid guide warned us of that danger, and that if we were caught, we would be sent back to Kiel and the authorities would charge us for attempting to flee. The irony of it is that, on the one hand, they did not want us to exist. On the other hand, they also did not want us to leave.

I am sure it was heartbreaking for my parents to say goodbye to my grandparents. They suspected that they might never see one another again, but they did what was best for us despite having to break up the family. My father's loyalty to his father, Alter Weber, must surely have been tested in the final hours before our departure.

I don't know how long the trek lasted. I was just four years old and my brother, Herbert, was two. At one point, I remember looking at the sky, and there was an enormous cloud that looked to me like God sitting on a sofa, leaning his upper torso toward me. I thought it was God, and I thought that God would protect us, because that is what I had learned from my mother and father and my grandfather. It was a comforting thought and allayed some of my fears. As is the case with so many children, I had my parents to look up to, and when a child has their parents, they feel protected. I would learn the truth of this when my brother and I were soon separated from my parents into the "arms of strangers." Being without my parents became one of the defining aspects of my life.

I don't recall other details of our journey. Maybe I fell asleep and my parents carried me, all the while looking out for local police, Nazis, and sympathizers who'd have gotten a charge out of intercepting and turning in wayward Jews. Or maybe the townsfolk saw us and knew exactly what we were doing and wished us well on our journey. Maybe some of them wished that they, too, could have left Germany. Or maybe they were glad to be rid of the "vermin," the Jews, and to confiscate what was left behind—furniture, empty apartments and houses, businesses and machinery, and stores and merchandise to sell.

Whatever the case was, we finally crossed the border into Belgium and settled for six months in Antwerp. My mother's sister and her family were already living there, which is perhaps one of the reasons we headed for Antwerp. It was a very important city in the time of war; it has a port where ships can load and unload men and munitions. Antwerp was also a wealthy city. It was, and still is, one of the centers of the global diamond trade. Many Jews are involved in the diamond business in Antwerp as diamond cutters and traders. Belgium's modern connection to diamonds is due in part to its own grisly history: its invasion of and domination over the Congo, where diamond mines and other natural resources were gobbled up under the direction of King Leopold. Whatever the sins of the Belgian people and monarchy may be, the country was good to us for a time. When we reached Antwerp there were about 50,000 Jews living in the city, many of whom had emigrated from eastern Europe.

My parents located an apartment with the help of a Jewish agency, and my father found employment. He had to have earned some money, because I do not know how much money they had with them. I am sure that they had to pay a great deal of money to the smugglers who took us into Belgium.

We left not a moment too soon. On September 1, 1939, the Germans launched a surprise attack against Poland, mobilizing armored tanks, fighter planes, and ground troops. The Poles fought back but were defeated within weeks. The world described the German attack as a blitzkrieg, or lightning attack. Britain and France stood by Poland. World War II was officially on.

* * *

For a while, life seemed normal to me, even if I was far from the Kiel harbor. I had my parents looking after my brother and me.

I remember going to an Orthodox synagogue in Antwerp. I was with my mother, of course, in the section reserved for women; the women and men did not pray together in the synagogue. They were separated in one form or another, even if only by a curtain. But in this synagogue, we sat upstairs in the balcony, overlooking the men sitting below us.

I remember that my mother and brother looked very happy. I think my mother was relieved to be back in the company of other Jews and performing ancient rituals in apparent safety. My father and mother exchanged glances and smiled at each other throughout the service. I am sure I was happy to see my parents relatively content after the struggles to flee Kiel and find safety in this sophisticated city.

My parents enrolled me in a religious preschool. Among other things, I was supposed to learn the Hebrew alphabet. I was always a stubborn kid. I don't know why, but I was. I wasn't a good student, and I didn't learn the Hebrew alphabet very well, but I remember the song. The "Aleph Bet" song, which was like "A, B, C..."

My father occasionally asked me what I learned about the alphabet, among other subjects. He was not thrilled with my answer, or lack of an answer. He knew I was a smart kid, so he must have chalked it up to laziness or indifference. He chastised me for not learning or for telling him the wrong answer to some questions that he thought should have been obvious. That was the first time my father got really mad at me for not learning my lessons. This would become a pattern. Looking back, he must have been under tremendous pressure and worried about what the future held, so his patience with me was short, and he expected a lot from me as his firstborn son.

He also did not like the way I ate. I chewed too loudly. I remember him telling me about this and I got angry, obstinate, and I would not budge. I would not talk to him, no matter how many times he tried to have a civil conversation with me. I remember a scene of my father sitting on a couch and me on the floor, brooding. My mother watched us but she did not interfere. I don't know if it was that she was afraid of my father's reaction, or that she anticipated we would resolve our differences.

Later when we immigrated to France, there were many instances when my father's tension and nervous stress made him act in a manner beyond his control. I became the target of his irritation, whereas Herbert, as the younger son, was without fault in my father's eyes. According to my father, as the older child, I was expected to behave correctly, to watch out, and do everything according to the family rules. I was to serve as an example of good behavior to my brother, but I did not like that role.

My father and I developed conflicts that set the stage for my rebellious nature as I got older. Despite our differences, I chose to remember my father as a very loving and caring man. In time, my mother did become my protector when my father let out his frustration on me, and she judged that he had gone too far. I am sure that these conflicts contributed to my anxiety as a child. I wonder if I ever asked my mother, "Why is Papa angry with me?" I think I just accepted his moodiness and hoped that my mother would intercede if he overreacted. I had no way to protect myself. I wouldn't dare hit my father or disrespect him. I'd just look at my mother with pleading eyes, hoping that she would rescue me.

One day as I was coming home from preschool by myself, I saw a strange sight: a funeral procession. There were horses draped in black and a chariot. The hearse was heavily decorated in black drapes as well. A long procession of men and women walking on foot followed the chariot in silence.

This was fascinating to me. I did not understand what this was about. I followed it for a while, and somehow I found my way back home. I am amazed to think that at the age of five-and-a-half, I was allowed to walk to and from Hebrew school by myself in a strange city. Perhaps my school was close to the place where we lived. I have no recollection of the addresses. Really, though, the dangers my family faced did not come from the streets of Antwerp. They came from Berlin. The Germans were plotting an attack against Belgium that would result in many citizens losing their lives or escaping for safety in whatever country would have them.

When I reached home, I described what I saw to my mother. I don't remember her exact explanation—whether she brought up the concept of death or explained this procession in some other way, perhaps as a solemn expression of duty to an important person, maybe nobility of some sort. This was the first time I had seen the outward manifestation of death, but I did not fully understand what it meant.

One time I was walking down from the second-floor apartment where we lived, and on the wall, I saw blood. I asked my father, "What is that?" He shielded my eyes and told me that an accident happened. I had never seen blood, not even when my mother fell from a chair hanging her drapes. I guess I saw blood when I hit my head on the corner table, but it couldn't have been much. But on the wall of the curved, downward staircase, there was a lot of blood.

My mother's sister and her husband visited us at our apartment. I liked my uncle very much. He used to sit me on his lap and joke with me. My aunt and uncle had three sons, and they were all very nice to Herb and me. They also had an older daughter, Adele [Mendelsohn], who was sent to Holland and hidden there by a Christian family. Later, she came to the United States to live with my great-uncle Max Fass in Oakland. She was one of the lucky survivors in our extended family.

One day, my mother's sister and her family came to our apartment building and called my mother to come downstairs. My mother and I went to the window, and my aunt said that they were leaving Antwerp and going to France. It was a very sad day for us, since they were the only family we had in the city. The war had started, and they were afraid that Antwerp would be directly in the line of fire because of its strategic port. If the Germans could destroy the port, it would cripple Belgium.

Germany had colluded with the Russians and created an excuse to attack Poland, which they did on September 1, 1939. That immediately triggered a treaty of defense among Poland, England, and France. We assumed they would soon attack the countries that were allied to Poland. This included Belgium. They were sure that the Germans would shortly attack places that could present a danger to their forces, either by land or sea. Antwerp certainly was one of those.

In 1936, Belgium's King Leopold III had declared neutrality with regard to Germany. He had hoped that neutrality, as opposed to open hostility, would dissuade Germany from invading Belgium again, as it had done during World War I. It was, of course, in Belgium that much of World War I had been fought, with nearly unimaginable carnage on all sides.

This neutrality strategy did not work. On May 10, 1940, the German army invaded Belgium, the Netherlands, and Luxembourg. The invasion was called Operation *Fall Gelb* ("Case Yellow"). The German Luftwaffe attacked the airport outside Antwerp and dropped bombs on the city's port. The Belgian army fought back but was overwhelmed by the invaders. Belgium surrendered on May 28, giving the invasion the name "18 Days' Campaign."

Belgium remained occupied by the Germans for the duration of World War II, and the Germans dictated to the Belgian people in what manner they should treat the Jews. Anti-Semitism was rife in Belgium, and the Jewish community was targeted for deportation and death. The Belgians generally cooperated with the Germans. Yet another country to jump to the commands of the puppet master—Hitler—and his minions with their loud voices, barking dogs, pistols and rifles, whips, and convoys of trucks rumbling through the city streets looking for Jews to shovel up, like so much snow during a blizzard.

My aunt and uncle and cousins fled Antwerp for Brittany on the French coast, which they deemed to be safer than Antwerp. The train they boarded was bombed by the Germans; my aunt and uncle and their sons did not survive the attack. They were the first of my family members to die at the hands of the Nazis. I found out about their deaths years later. I am sure that my parents did not share this terrible news with my brother and me. It is one of those moments when fate intervened and my family was saved. Had we gone with them, we surely would have been killed on that train.

I don't know why my mother's sister was unable to convince my mother that we should leave with them, but *grâce à Dieu*, we stayed behind. (Many years later, my aunt's daughter, Adele, together with her own daughter wrote an autobiography about her wartime experiences and about the fate that befell her family.)

Shortly after my aunt, uncle, and their sons departed, our family boarded a train going south with hundreds of Belgians who also were fleeing the country to avoid the bombings. Christians, Jews, anyone—they were all fleeing to France, a country that temporarily allowed refugees to enter without complications.

In this particular case, our train went to the southwest part of France, stopping in the city of Marmande in the Department of Lot-et-Garonne. The trip was more than 804 kilometers traveling through France. We disembarked from the train. I looked around at a strange city where people spoke a language I did not really understand. (People in Antwerp spoke Dutch and some French, but how much of their French I understood as a little boy I have no recollection.) Everyone who stepped off the train with their suitcases and precious memorabilia needed to find a place to live. My mother carried with her a box in which she kept important family documents, photographs, and the like, which she held on to throughout the war years. This box would become a treasure trove of memories and events that helped me to piece together some of what happened to my family.

It was May 1940, just before my sixth birthday, when we arrived in Marmande with other refugee families. Where were we going to live? What was my father going to do to support us? Would I have to go to school? Where would I make friends? Would I see more bloodshed? Life was full of unknowns, which added to my inherent anxiety. But then I'd look into my mother's kind and compassionate eyes and feel the touch of her warm hand on my brow, brushing my hair back, and I'd feel better.

With my parents and my baby brother Herbert at the beach in Kiel.

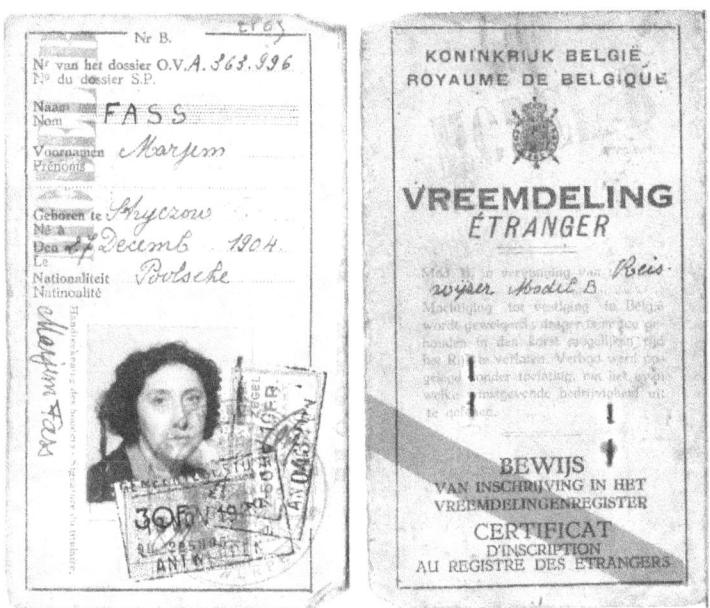

My mother's entry card to Belgium.

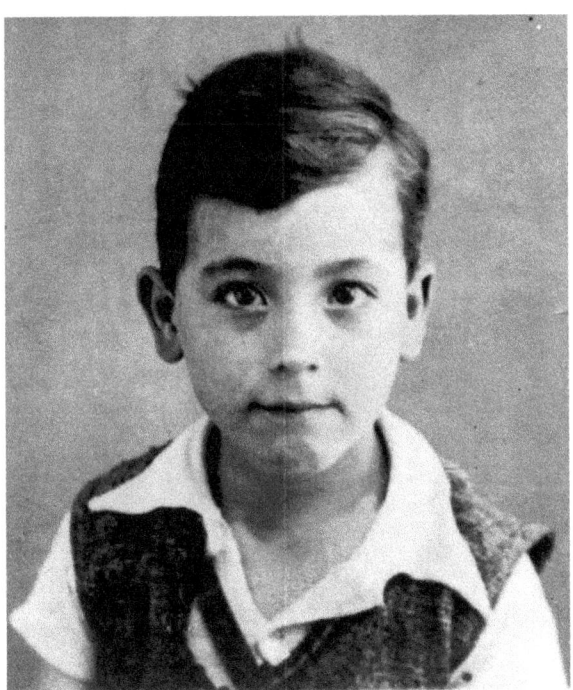

At age 6 or 7, taken in Belgium or France, perhaps by school officials.

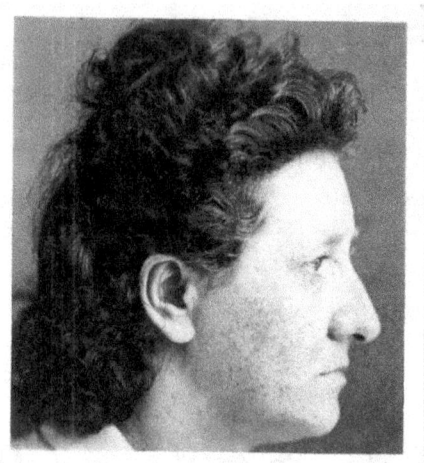

Identification photographs of my mother and my father, 1943, Marjem and Simche Lakritz, taken in France, by Vichy authorities. All emigrants had to carry identification cards.

CHAPTER 4

A Safe Haven

The town of Marmande, in the Department of Lot-et-Garonne, is in southwest France near Agen. Founded in the twelfth century by Richard the Lionheart, it is on the southern railway line, which connects Bordeaux to Sète and has, historically, been the site of a key crossing of the Garonne River, which flows from Spain to France and into the Atlantic Ocean.

This Department lays claim to some of the finest tomatoes in all of France, if not the world.

The mild climate and rich soil are perfect for growing almost any kind of vegetable. Midway between Bordeaux to the northwest and Toulouse to the southeast, it grows its own variety of grapes and is known for its cognac and Armagnac. Farmers raise dairy cattle, chickens, and ducks. Its foie gras is among the best in the world. The crops of the region are sold in Paris and served in its Michelin-starred restaurants. They helped make Paris the culinary capital of France and France the culinary capital of the world.

I remember the tomatoes. They were excellent in texture and taste. They were the platonic ideal of what a tomato is supposed to taste like.

We arrived by train in Marmande on May 17, 1940, according to my mother's *carte valable,* just before the Vichy government was installed in the spa town of Vichy in central France. My mother was thirty-six years old, and my father three years younger. Had events in Europe been different, my parents would probably have been leading the comfortable life of a young couple in Kiel, looking forward to watching their sons mature, taking holidays in the mountains and by the seashore somewhere, and building a healthy nest egg. Instead, they were grateful that all of us were alive and beyond the immediate reach of German tanks and troops.

For the first few nights our family and other refugees slept in an agricultural warehouse on the Boulevard de Mare, named after a prominent nobleman or general—typical of many street names throughout France.

An aid agency must have helped us secure proper housing. Our home in Marmande was an apartment on the second floor of a small building. It was around the corner from a tomato factory, which produced tomato sauce, tomato paste, and whatever other tomato products you could imagine. It was a shame that they pulverized those fresh, flavorful Dordogne tomatoes only to alter their flavor and make them unrecognizable. Then again, Dordogne had tomatoes to spare.

When we fled from Belgium, we went in the only direction we could. But even if we'd had a choice, France made sense. Among countries we feasibly could have traveled to, France was the best of bad options. The Franco regime in Spain was officially neutral but shared fascistic sympathies with Italy and Germany. And, of course, the legacy of the Spanish Inquisition hung over many European Jews. Portugal was too far, and England and Scandinavia would have required boat trips. Fascist Italy was aligned with the Nazis.

Roughly a month after Belgium's surrender, facing a German invasion, France negotiated an armistice that was enacted on June 22, 1940, a month after we arrived in Marmande. Under the terms of the armistice, the northern and central part of France became German-occupied territories. The Germans gained the industrial north and the large segment of production of farm products, and in the middle of France they gained control of the coast facing England and the Atlantic. They allowed the French to rule under the dominion and supervision of the German government in the southern portion of France in what was called the Vichy occupation zone with its own head of state and government, separate from the rest of the country. The Vichy government controlled Marmande and the surrounding cities, towns, and villages.

The Vichy government was headed by Marshal Pétain, who was a World War I hero, He was assisted by a Frenchman called François Darlan, an anti-Semite and a terrible person in other respects, and by former Prime Minister Pierre Laval, who collaborated willingly with the Nazis. Pétain was a very old man, and I am sure he had dementia; they used him as a puppet figurehead to basically make a pretense that France had some form of independence. Among Pétain's many gestures of fealty to the Nazis, he organized the Commissariat général aux questions juives ("General Commissariat for Jewish Questions") in March 1941. As implied by its ominously bureaucratic name, the CGQJ became one of the means by which the Nazi "final solution" to the "Jewish problem" was carried out in France.

You might think that Marmande, which had a population of about 15,000 at the time, would be insulated from the politics and violence of the Nazi invasion. It was not. It's true that no battles were waged there. But the war forced all free people to take a side, even tomato farmers far from the front lines. Those citizens who opposed the Nazis did so risking their lives. Even when they were against the Nazis, they pretended to cooperate.

The police and the Catholic Church both ostensibly supported the Vichy government. The people of Marmande believed that the arrangements made to establish a Vichy government would guarantee protection from a German invasion. Among the edicts that local government officials were expected to fulfill was to keep meticulous records of the Jewish refugees: their names, where they resided, and what work they did to contribute to the economy of Lot-et-Garonne, whether they were city laborers, farmers' assistants, street sweepers, seamstresses, cooks.

There was a formal line of demarcation between the "Free French" territory of Vichy and the German occupied zone. Sentries were posted along the line to control people from crossing from one section to another. "The occupation authorities carried out rigorous surveillance along the demarcation line, which could only be crossed with permission at official crossing points on presenting an identity card and an Ausweis (free pass) issued by the Kommandanturen (German authority offices responsible for the military and civil administration of a particular zone). Any request had to be accompanied by a complete file submitted to the German authorities, including identity photographs, an address certificate and the reason for the request." [2]

The most prestigious building in Marmande was the Gothic cathedral Église de Notre Dame de Marmande. Constructed in the fourteenth century and enlarged and completed in the seventeenth century, it mirrors the style of the greatest Gothic cathedrals such as Notre Dame de Paris, but on a smaller scale. It has a rose window, a stump of a steeple to the left of the rose window, and, at the other end of the apse, a bell tower topped by a decorative dome.

Catholicism features prominently in the history of Marmande, as it does in the overall history of France. I think of cathedrals as ideal metaphors for Catholicism. They are beautiful, just as there are beautiful things about Catholic teachings and many Catholic people—including many who helped and loved me throughout my childhood. But those cathedrals were built with slave labor and paid for by a corrupt, opulent clergy with the blessing of the reigning monarchy at the time. This is the side of Catholicism that colluded with the Nazis and willingly adopted policies against Jewish immigrants.

But Marmande was not particularly Catholic, as far as I can recall. Some people went to church, and others did not. Marmande did not have a synagogue. Services were generally held privately in homes owned by the few citizen Jews living in Marmande at the time. Eventually, there would be a schism between the native Jews who saw themselves as assimilated with the general population and those Jews—like my family—who had emigrated from Germany and eastern Europe. They were seen as outsiders and the authorities treated them with disdain. It did not

[2] heminsdememoire.gouv.fr/en/demarcation-line-1940-1944.

take much to persuade the police and public officials to cooperate with the Nazis against these Jewish outsiders.

Over the centuries, Jews were forced to band together for their own protection in many European cities and often lived in ghettos at the direction of the governments in power. Post-revolutionary France was far more egalitarian. The French Republic allowed Jews to live freely and, mostly, equally with people of other backgrounds. Dating back to the reign of Napoleon, France gave Jews the right of citizenship. Napoleon was a great man in that respect. He broke from the Catholic Church the way he broke with so many other traditions. He appreciated the social contributions of Jews in business, scholarship, and so on.

But anti-Semitism was not swept aside by the Enlightenment following the French Revolution or Napoleon's "enlightened edicts." In 1894, a French artillery officer of Jewish ancestry, Army Captain Alfred Dreyfus, was falsely accused of treason. He was sentenced to penal servitude. The Dreyfus affair became one of the most polarizing incidents in the history of France. The famous writer and journalist Émile Zola published an open letter accusing the president and the French government of judicial errors and lack of evidence against Monsieur Dreyfus. His letter, "J'Accuse," appeared on the front page of the newspaper, *L'Aurore*. The case ended with Dreyfus's exoneration after protracted trials.

My parents perceived France as a Jewish-tolerant country, even if it had relatively few native Jews compared to Germany, Poland, and other eastern European countries. All we wanted at the time, though, was to get away from the bombing. And Marmande was hundreds of kilometers from the nearest German tank, military maneuver, or air raid.

Many other families had the same idea. Before World War II, France had fewer than 200,000 Jewish citizens. As refugees like us flooded in, France's Jewish population, including citizens and refugees alike, swelled to around 320,000, of whom 150,000 were foreign born. These were persons most vigorously targeted by the Vichy government under the direction of the Germans.

* * *

When we arrived in France, we were nearly destitute. We had nothing. We had no money, with only the clothes on our backs. We had the few utensils that my parents acquired in Marmande to make food, and that is all. It's hard to say whether the French government was welcoming. Perhaps "tolerant" is the appropriate word. As noncitizens, in a country under the thumb of the Germans, it was the best we could hope for. And where else could we have gone?

We were considered stateless people since we had no visa from Germany; we were not citizens of Belgium, and we had no official status in France. So as "illegals," we were granted a temporary visa to stay in Marmande. Every thirty days my parents had to go to the police station to renew their temporary permits.

If someone was caught with an expired identity card or no identity card at all, they would be imprisoned by the Vichy government. My parents did as the law required. The local government of Marmande knew where we lived, who we were, our ages, and what we were doing. They could exercise power of dominion over us in any manner that they chose. But we were safe, at least in the short-term until the Nazis put the squeeze on the Vichy government to come after the immigrant Jews in their midst.

The apartment where we eventually found shelter in Marmande was in a narrow, beautiful old building made of mud, straw, and wood, dating back to the Middle Ages on the Boulevard de Mare. We lived in a small upstairs apartment without electricity. The downstairs was used as a garage; it had been a horse stable for most of its existence. The building was in the poor district of the town, in a working-class neighborhood with small houses surrounding it, nothing like the wealthier section of Marmande with well-appointed apartments and spacious houses, where affluent Jews of French descent lived.

My father became known by the refugee Jews as a pious and religious man. As he had done in Kiel, he conducted religious services in our apartment. I remember him blowing the shofar to mark the beginning of the New Year and the Day of Atonement. As he had done every day of his adult life, he recited the Amidah morning, afternoon, and evening, wrapping the leather tefillin in which a copy of the prayer is housed:

Bless us, our Father, one and all, with the light of Your face. For by the light of Your face you have given us, Lord our God, a Torah of life and love of kindness, charity, blessing, mercy, life, and peace. May it please You to bless Your people Israel at all times and in every hour with Your peace.

I wonder what my father thought as he recited this prayer. Hope must have been the operative sentiment.

We lived in that apartment in Marmande for about a year and a half. Our neighbor was Secrétaire Général de Mairie Gérard Guillot. He played an important role in the fate of my mother and father as you will learn.

My father worked as a day laborer for the town of Marmande and for the farmers in surrounding areas who needed help during the harvest. He also worked for other employers who took enormous advantage of him. They knew they could get away with it because of his desperate circumstances and the fact that he had no one in authority who would listen to his complaints and care. The local authorities had no sympathy for the immigrants. The only laws that applied to immigrants were the restrictive laws and criminal laws, not laws of freedom and true justice.

Some of the people who hired him paid barely a living wage to support a family of four. But they often allowed him to take food, including the vegetables and fruits that grew in abundance on the farms in the region. He brought home this produce for my mother to prepare meals for us so we didn't starve.

Living close to farms gave us some access to food, whereas citizens living in large cities such as Paris had to import all of their supplies and were probably confronted with many more scarcities of food and fuel. That is perhaps why so many people fled to the countryside, where food would be plentiful and families could be relatively self-sufficient. Marmande was spared the boots of the Nazis marching through the streets, spying on the population, and looking for Jews to arrest and deport—at least in the beginning of the war.

I observed in Marmande a big *fête*, a festival whereby generals and other bureaucrats of the Vichy government came to tell the people, in an environment of music and speeches, that all was well. The administrator of Lot-et-Garonne Préfecture in a public speech told everyone that France was cooperating with Germany for the betterment of Europe, and that the current division of France into occupied France and Vichy France was a temporary arrangement. He urged the citizens to have patience and remain loyal to France and to its government in Vichy, guaranteeing that the Germans would not interfere with the Vichy government and all would be well. This propaganda was spread throughout the streets, on the radio, and by dignitaries who spoke at the *fête*. Of course, the French had made a deal with the devil, because the Vichy government turned out to be nothing more than a puppet of the Germans.

The city gave my father the job of erecting viewing stands around the square for the *fête*, which took place on the Boulevard de Mare, near our apartment. He must have been very strong to carry the planks and pipes that were used to construct the stands.

People turned out to listen to the speeches. Whether they believed what they were being told, I have no idea, but they certainly believed that cooperating with the Nazis was better than being embroiled in a war that they thought they would have no chance of winning. They consoled themselves with the illusion that the Vichy government was run by their French compatriots. Some citizens must have wondered what had happened to the constitution that French men and women had spilled blood to create in 1792, ending the monarchy. Perhaps they could look to London, where General Charles de Gaulle had established the headquarters of Free France, fighting against the Germans and struggling to reinstate what the French Revolution accomplished almost 200 years earlier—liberty, equality, fraternity. Through his radio broadcasts from London, General Charles de Gaulle supported the French resistance and spoke out against Pétain, who condemned de Gaulle to death in absentia. On July 10, 1941, Pétain asserted the power to revise the French constitution. He granted himself powers to initiate a "national revolution."

Thereafter, the French government took increasingly aggressive steps, as had occurred in Germany, to deny Jews of their civil rights and property rights. They were identified in their legal documents with a big letter *J* identifying them as Jews. This practice was adopted at the international Évian Conference of 1938, in which thirty-two countries agreed to appease the German government and identify the Jews by marking their passports and visas with a letter *J*, making it easier to round them up or prohibit them entry to one country or another. The United States sent a representative to the Évian Conference. The subtext of the entire conference was to appease Germany and restrain it from further military action, which turned out to be futile.

As the war progressed, if Jews—refugees or native born—tried to leave France, they had to provide the following to the authorities: an entry visa to the desired overseas country; a bank guarantee in the host country; and a place on a ship, which might cost $400 per person, the passage to be paid either by the passenger or by a Jewish organization referred to as HICEM.[3] Very few Jews were lucky enough to furnish the necessary exit documents.

In many towns of this region, anti-Semitism reared its ugly head. In neighboring Agen, Jews were accused of killing their neighbor's poultry by feeding them corn with pins stuck into them. In Penne, someone was recorded to have told a Jewish person, "You have no horns. You cannot be a Jew." When a family by the name of Nathan arrived in a small town, the mayor asked them, "Excuse me, do you have forked feet?" Jews were accused of driving up the prices of produce by "engaging in

---

[3] HICEM was an organization established in 1927 whose goal was to help European Jews emigrate. HICEM was formed with the merger of three Jewish migration associations: HIAS (Hebrew Immigrant Aid Society), which was based in New York; ICA (Jewish Colonization Association), which was based in Paris but registered as a British charitable society; and Emigdirect, a migration organization based in Berlin. The name HICEM is an acronym of HIAS, ICA, and Emigdirect.

bargaining at exaggerated prices," reflecting what was alleged in Vichy propaganda.[4]

Even in this climate, Jews felt safer in the Lot-et-Garonne region than in the German-occupied zone to the north, where any day a Nazi official might knock on someone's door and drag them away to their death. The flow of arrivals in Lot-et-Garonne increased as of May 1942 when the wearing of the Star of David on their clothing became mandatory in the French-occupied zone to the north, and even more so after the July 1942 roundups.

* * *

I was enrolled in one of Marmande's public schools. I stayed there only for a month. In that school, I remember not speaking French very well and not being accustomed to being in school at all. The only school I had attended was a Hebrew preschool in Antwerp, which I did not like. There I was a reluctant student and engendered my father's wrath because I refused to learn my ABCs.

I remember learning the French poem about the tortoise and the hare by La Fontaine. One ran around and frolicked and had fun, and the other one saved for the months of winter and hunger: "While the slow Tortoise creeps / Mister Hare makes four leaps / And then loafs around in the sun." I also remember when I had to go to the bathroom, and we were required to raise our hands in class for permission. I did as I was told, and the teacher was busy talking to another student and either didn't see me or deliberately ignored me, although I was jumping up and down,

---

[4] Marie-Juliette Vielcazat-Petitcol, *Lot-et-Garonne: Land of Exile, Land of Asylum: The Jewish Refugees During World War II*, trans. Sylvia Brandon-Perez (Narrosse: Albret, 2006), 229–232.

trying not to wet my pants. I became desperate. She finally acknowledged me and sent me to the bathroom before I embarrassed myself in front of all the other children in my class.

After school, I was encouraged to hunt for snails by a nice lady who lived around the corner from us. She promised to pay me if I collected snails for her. That must be the first time I ever earned any money. I am sure that my parents were very happy with me for doing a responsible thing like that. I was not going to "loaf around in the sun" like the hare.

CHAPTER 5

Love Thy Neighbor as Thyself

One of the bureaucratic practices governing refugee Jews in France was that the local officials could essentially move Jewish families around whenever they wanted in order to keep a close eye on them. Native-born Jews were generally allowed to stay in their homes and run their businesses as usual for a time. Foreign-born Jews were subjected to a system of arbitrary relocation from the day they arrived.

At some point, my family had to leave our apartment in Marmande. We did not go far. We moved to the hamlet of Saint-Pardoux-du-Breuil, three or four kilometers away. We carried what little clothing and possessions we had, and my mother held her box of remembrances tightly along the path.

Saint-Pardoux-du-Breuil, which is usually shortened to Saint-Pardoux (not to be confused with several other towns named Saint-Pardoux throughout France), has a beautiful church and a bar, and all around the hamlet were farms that grew the plentiful produce the region was known for. Saint-Pardoux was like a picture postcard of what one imagines the French countryside to look like: rolling hills, fields full of sunflowers, vineyards, and more. It was located over 500 kilometers from Paris, a truly out-of-the-way place, but still under the watchful eye of local authorities who sympathized with the Nazis and were more than willing to follow their directives. As the war escalated, the eradication of the Jews intensified. The "final solution" was articulated at the Wannsee Conference on January 20, 1942. More than 44,000 incarceration and death factories were built mainly in Germany and Poland to exterminate the Jews. But that was still to come.

My parents obtained housing in an annex farm building in Saint-Pardoux. It was a rectangular building, divided by a wall down the middle. On one side was room for storage, and the other side was reserved for the cows who, morning and night, would be brought into their stalls for milking. The rest of the day they grazed in the fields.

My family ended up in the storage part of this building. It had a window to let in air, but it was so small, there was almost no light, nor was there a fireplace for heat. It had a dirt floor and one door. Some of the helpers on the farm gave us a few pieces of furniture to use. We got our water from a well, and light was furnished by kerosene lamps.

There was a little garden on the side of the building. My father was given permission by the owners to grow vegetables in this area, which he did. I believe that this was granted to us at no cost.

The people who loaned us this half of the building were interesting people. The owner of the building was Henri Berney, the village blacksmith—a *forgeron*. He and his family were devout Catholics, so much so that their son was in seminary training for the priesthood. I am sure, from their point of view, they took us in as an act of charity, religious duty, and goodness. That is one of the many paradoxes of my story—that there were people who showed us the utmost compassion and kindness and others whose wickedness and depravity knew no bounds.

The *forgeron,* as his name implies, made and repaired agricultural tools, as well as horseshoes. He also helped my father find work as a day laborer on different farms so that he could earn a living. Their shop was across the street from where we stayed. Many years later, when I visited Saint-Pardoux, he told me that I was a precocious, interesting, lively, good child. I am glad that this is the impression he had of me. Whether I deserved it or not, I do not know.

The place that became our home had been a sanctuary for families fleeing the Spanish Civil War from 1938–39. When the fascist Franco prevailed, they returned home, so the barn was now vacant. My father cultivated a garden, using his own excrement as fertilizer for our food that he grew. I am not sure how he knew how to farm since he had lived in a city for much of his adulthood. Perhaps someone showed him what to do to make the most of the plot that was offered to him. He was a hard worker, a very strong, sturdy individual, and certainly he was going to do anything and everything to see that his family was protected. That is why he kept himself in good health, with proper nourishment.

While we were living in Saint-Pardoux my mother became a seamstress to earn a few francs. She learned to sew as a young girl, and she was good at it. She started making clothing for the farmers. One farmer would recommend her to another farm family, asking her for different types of clothing for young children and adults, and of course she learned their styles.

One of the families that she met in this way was the Ros family. Jeanne and Pierre Ros were immigrants from northern Italy, just over the border from France near the Dolomites. They had left Italy during a famine. They, like many other Italians in that region, couldn't make a living in agriculture. A good Catholic family, they had a lot of children. They immigrated and settled in the area of Saint-Pardoux, where they became tenant farmers on land that belonged to the Baronesse de Ferrier au chateau de Cuq.[5] That was a common way for poor farmers to get by: they would work the land for the owner, and in return they were allowed to eat some of the food they picked and harvested along with some payment for the crops they grew for the Baronesse. It was similar to the feudal system that had prevailed in medieval Europe hundreds of years earlier, or the sharecropping of the post-Civil War American South. The family raised tobacco, plums, and peaches. They also had a big vineyard and made wine that they sold on behalf of the Baronesse.

What also felt medieval was that all the farming was done by hand or with animals, such as mules, pulling tractors since gasoline and oil were scarce during the war. Horse-drawn carriages were also used for transportation. Living in Saint-Pardoux in such bucolic surroundings, it was hard for us to imagine that a war was being waged with modern equipment like tankers, airplanes, battleships, and chemicals, while we got by with the sweat of our own labor and the strength of horses, mules, and rudimentary tools.

---

[5] Cuq is a commune in the Lot-et-Garonne department in southwestern France with about 300 inhabitants.

Saint-Pardoux was as peaceful as it was rustic. We depended on the charity and goodness of others, but we never received a handout. We had to earn everything. My father worked hard to plant and harvest and assist the farmers. They benefited from his work. My mother did the same as a seamstress. I am sure that many days they felt like giving up, but they had two young sons to take care of, so even in their darkest days they never ceased struggling. And they, in turn, benefited from the kindness of neighbors who regarded the Lakritz family as good people, worthy of aid and succor. If you had asked them why they helped us, they would probably have answered, "It is the right thing to do."

I was asked by a lady in our neighborhood to collect wild herbs, and she paid me just as I had been paid for collecting snails. I think she singled me out because I was the child of refugees and she wanted to help us in some way without simply giving us a handout that would have made us all feel like charity cases. While there is nothing wrong with charity, it is far better for the soul to earn your keep than to be given a handout. She would be one of many villagers of Saint-Pardoux who helped us to survive.

When we moved to Saint-Pardoux I was enrolled in the local school. Every morning we stood around under a flagpole flying the French tricolor. We had to pledge allegiance to the Vichy government and sing "La Marseillaise," the French national anthem. At the time, I went along with it. I had never developed a sense of citizenship in Germany or in Belgium, so these gestures didn't mean much to me. I didn't feel as if I was being disloyal to a true homeland. In fact, home to me was defined by where my parents were. It was more of a psychological and spiritual place than a place defined by borders. To the French, though, they were intent on upholding the pretense that their part of the country under Vichy rule was still independent and not occupied or controlled by the Germans.

That was a farce, of course. The occupation was done with the cooperation of the French government and many French people, who were willing to give up their country's soul for the sake of avoiding a full German invasion. It was considered a necessary accommodation to save lives and protect their country from destruction. Eventually this rapprochement would not work. As the Germans became more depraved and greedier, France's treasures were pillaged, its cities, towns, and villages were sacked, and its people were murdered, most especially its immigrant Jews.

My parents lived in a state of dislocation, anxiety, and fear. They were not allowed to obtain regular employment without the permission of the police. They had to have an identity card or they were subject to arrest at any time.

Under these conditions my father's mood swings became more severe, and he took his anger out on me. But I hasten to add that most of the time he was a tender and loving father and did his best to take care of us. It was just one trauma piled on top of another that brought my father to the breaking point almost daily.

My mother was rarely angry with me but for one occasion. Before we were forced to move to the village of Saint-Pardoux, I was walking with a French girl whom I had met in school and loitered with her outside our apartment in Marmande on the Boulevard du Mare. I was happy to have a friend. My mother saw me from the window, and when I went upstairs, she was furious, screaming and yelling, "Alfred, how can you be speaking to a *shiksa*?" I didn't know that this word meant she was not a

Jewish girl, nor did I know that I was breaking some rule by being friendly with her.

I don't know what got into my mother's head. She took a broom and she hit me with it. I was hurt and startled by her anger. I was just an innocent little boy and did not deserve such harsh treatment. That experience taught me that I would never treat my children that way for any reason whatsoever, whether they were right or wrong.

From her perspective, she was trying to keep her child from making a lifelong mistake. I guess my mother felt that intermarriages did not result in happiness for the couple or for their children, and to her, the war only underscored this reality. After all, it was the Christians who had abandoned us—Nazis openly despised us, and other Christians stood by and watched their cruelty toward us, although there were some who were kind and took pity on us. That is one of the mysteries of humanity: that some people choose the path of love and others choose the path of hate.

My father began to learn French, but I don't know how fluent he was. I know this through Joseph Delnegro, the son-in-law of the Ros family. As Joseph told me, my father would go to their farm and socialize with his father. Apparently, Monsieur Delnegro, Sr. was one of the few people in the village who spoke German, so if my father did not know a word in French, he could say it in German.

All of those years of education that I should have had—if not preschool and kindergarten, at least first grade on—I didn't attend, except for sporadic episodes. When life was peaceful in Saint-Pardoux, I went regularly, for weeks on end. But all the moving around, plus the language barrier, meant that my education was not remotely comprehensive or stable.

The school I attended in Saint-Pardoux was a two-room schoolhouse on a street near where we lived at the time. The different grades must all have been in just these two rooms. How much the children learned, I don't really know. I did learn to count with wooden sticks and rubber bands in packets of ten, and we would have to separate them into numbered groups. It was very rudimentary.

The local children were cruel. They taunted me and tied me to the gate along the back fence of the schoolhouse. They said they were going to crucify me like the Jews crucified Jesus Christ. I had no knowledge of Jesus Christ other than seeing His image on a cross at the front of the schoolroom, there to remind everyone that He was watching over us and protecting those who believed in Him. I remember this incident vividly, which is perhaps one of the reasons I developed a dislike for school.

The Catholic priests taught their congregants that Jews were Christ-killers. They elaborated this story by telling them that Jews needed the blood of Christians to make matzoh—the unleavened bread eaten by Jews during the Passover seder. Many Catholics believed that if a priest said something, it must be true. On the other hand, there were Christians living in Saint-Pardoux who were sympathetic to the plight of the Jews, since they were themselves in the minority, with France being predominantly a Catholic country. People made choices of what and whom to believe, and those beliefs governed their actions toward those who needed their help. One of the difficulties Jews encountered was knowing whom to trust. Someone might have appeared friendly, while secretly gathering information to share with the authorities, pointing a finger to curry favors and earn them material gain.

I did learn the French language in school as well as the patois, which is the local dialect spoken among farmers and other rural people. They were not formally educated and did not learn the French language in school. That is why they developed their own language, which incorporated French with their own expressions and words.

Meanwhile, I completely forgot what little German I knew. I refused to learn another word. Later in my life, after the war, my mother would speak German with others. I would not learn it, speak it, remember it, or understand it. It wasn't just a matter of being stubborn. It was a reflection of my deep-seated feelings toward the Nazis in particular, and Germany in general, and what they had done to us and to the millions of Jews whom they murdered.

My brother, Herbert, and I had a few playmates in Saint-Pardoux. Across the street from where we lived, there was a bar, and the barkeeper had one son. I lost his name and have only faint memories of him. However, on my visit to Saint-Pardoux in September 2000 with my family, someone introduced me, out of the blue, to this man whose name and existence I had forgotten. There he was, still living in the same house. He reminded me of childhood events in Saint-Pardoux that had long since faded from my memory.

Next to the barn was the house where his grandmother had lived and kept three or four cows. These cows were housed between her home and our barn. He told me that I would go and visit the cows and watch the milking. I probably even helped a little bit. I was very curious and interested in all these things.

I also remember the blacksmith's open forge, which was across the street. I would often watch him make horseshoes. He also fixed axes and plows so that they could burr the ground for planting. He was very nice to me, and so was his wife, and I am grateful for their charity, for their respect, for their tolerance and compliance with their own religious teachings. This was a family of true Christians, who did not merely follow their religious principles and duties to their church and their culture, but were tolerant and giving to strangers and members of different religious groups. They were an example of people who followed one of the Ten Commandments: "Love thy neighbor as thyself." If this was truly a part of their theological doctrine, how could some people be so cruel, willingly exposing the Jews in their midst, when they knew what the outcome would be?

The blacksmith's son told me how frustrated his parents were by their inability to help my parents. They were very much aware of the state of anxiety under which my father and mother were living. They were in constant fear of the knock on the door. My mother told me that my father had at one time altered his appearance, growing a mustache so he would not be recognized by German soldiers if they happened to come by and remembered him from Kiel. That would have been impossible, but in retrospect it is obvious that my father suffered from warranted paranoia.

One day my mother asked me to take lunch to my father in the fields. He was sweating profusely from working in the hot sun, and he had a thick beard. When he saw me, he reached out and hugged me fiercely and thanked me. I felt his love. I will always recall his strong arms around me and his kind eyes. Perhaps we sat down and talked father-to-son about nothing in particular in a way that did not reveal his fear that we might be separated at any time. He tried to maintain an air of normalcy, knowing that at any moment he might be arrested.

There were many French citizens who acted directly against Jews by denying them employment, income, and housing, who turned them over to the French police who then handed them off to the Nazis. Then there were others who were totally indifferent and did not lift a finger to help them. By doing nothing they were condemning the Jews to death. And then there were the outright collaborationists who loudly proclaimed: "All to the stake, dirty Jews. To death, dirty Yids."

Despite all of this, my parents did not give up hope.

During the war my father (sometimes accompanied by my mother) secretly met with other Jews in Lot-et-Garonne who were part of the Jewish underground. There was also a larger French Resistance movement—made up of a broader mix of people— that was referred to as the Maquis or the "Army of Shadows."[6] Both groups often worked in concert with one another against the Nazis.

In the dark of the night, my father rode his bicycle to a designated meeting area, hid in a ditch, and watched for two bicycle lights signaling the whereabouts of others who were gathering somewhere to plan. Their jobs were mainly to intercept messages from the Germans to learn of their battle maneuvers. My father became the local leader of the Jewish underground in

---

[6] *Army of Shadows* is the title of a film made by Jean-Pierre Melville, who was a member of the Resistance. He portrayed the minds of the Resistance members as those who must live with constant fear, persist in the face of futility, accept the deaths of their comrades, and expect no reward, except the knowledge that they are doing the right thing. Because many died under false names, their sacrifices are never known.

the Lot-et-Garonne territory, which had its main headquarters in Toulouse.

These were small acts, located far from where the full horrors of the war were taking place, but my mother and father must have felt that they were secretly doing something to contribute to the Resistance. How many people in Saint-Pardoux knew what they were up to is unknown, but their efforts would eventually lead to catastrophe. That my parents participated in the "Army of Shadows" attests to their bravery in the face of almost certain death.

My brother and I knew nothing of their activities but would learn about it when my father was honored years later as a hero of the Resistance, and my mother was given a pension by the French government as the widow of a war hero.

CHAPTER 6

Summer Camp

When I had just celebrated my eighth birthday in June and my brother was almost five, our parents announced to us that we were being sent away to a summer camp. They shared this news with us in such a way that we thought it was a privilege, emphasizing the freedom we would have in the countryside, the opportunity to play with other Jewish boys, and the chance to leave the confines of Saint-Pardoux. It was June 1942.

In truth, my parents were attempting to keep us out of harm's way. There were rumors that my parents were being spied on and might become the targets of a sweep to move immigrant Jews to prison. They deemed that summer camp would keep us safe. The camp was sponsored by a Jewish organization called Œuvre de Secours aux Enfants (OSE) which means, literally, "Work for the Security of Children" and was usually translated as "Society for Rescuing Children."[7]

---

[7] OSE was founded in 1912 by doctors in Saint Petersburg, Russia, as Obshchetsvo Zdravookhraneniya Yevreyiev ("Organization for the health protection of Jews"—OZE), to help needy members of the Jewish population. Branches were established in

Herbert and I traveled by train to summer camp. I remember being at the railroad station in Marmande, being delivered to the train by my father and mother. I remember being aboard the train and looking through the window at my parents, waving cheerfully and with an abundance of love. It was our first separation from our parents. I remember my father's smiling face as he and my mother stood on the platform with other parents sending their precious children off to camp for what we were told would be a two-week stay.

I am sure that my parents emphasized that I should watch out for my younger brother. I felt as if I was having my childhood taken away from me—to be responsible for another child meant that I myself could no longer be a child. I promised my parents that I would be an obedient son and look after Herbert. This was my duty.

They kissed us and waved goodbye. It would be the last time I would ever see my father.

The camp was headed by Monsieur le Directeur Cohn. Everything was done for the benefit of us children, including giving us some Jewish education through prayer and observance of Jewish holidays. We ate communal meals and played games.

There was a large map that included "Palestine," painted in blue and white with little lights behind it, that was displayed in one of the communal rooms as a visual reminder of our Jewish faith and heritage. The camp administrators wanted all the children to maintain their Jewish identity.

other countries. In 1923 the organization relocated to Berlin. In 1933, fleeing Nazism, it relocated again, this time to France, where it became the Œuvre de Secours aux Enfants ("Society for Rescuing Children"), retaining a similar acronym. In France, the OSE ran children's homes (often called "châteaux," but actually large mansions). These homes were for Jewish children of various ages, including infants. Many of their parents were either in Nazi concentration camps or had been killed.

Being in summer camp was fun for Herbert and me. There were, I suppose, maybe forty or fifty children and older teenagers and adults in this summer camp. On the Shabbos, though, we were not allowed to engage in any activities that would be construed as work. I remember being tossed in the air from a blanket sling held by others. It was fun. Children like this feeling of flying through the air.

After about two weeks at the camp, some of the children were sent home. We saw them packing up their suitcases and being taken back to the railroad station to be reunited with their parents. I am sure I wondered if my brother and I were going home as well. I certainly missed my parents, but I was also having a good time in the countryside and enjoyed playing games and running around.

My brother and I were called into Monsieur Cohn's office. We stood in front of his desk, and he explained to my brother and me that he had received a letter from my father. He showed us the letter, which was addressed to Herr Directeur Cohn and dated 30 Aug 1942 and written in German. (I have his letter among my documents.)

Monsieur Cohn had the difficult task of telling us that our parents wanted us to stay at camp past the time that we were expected to return to Saint-Pardoux.

I asked, "Why can't we go home?"

He hesitated and then confessed, "Well, it is for your protection; it is for their protection." Of course, I could not comprehend this. My brother, at his age, could not comprehend anything. Years later when he was asked to describe his experiences at this camp, he simply repeated what I had told him.

He had no memory of that time between June and September 1942.

Following the roundup of Jews in greater Paris, some 7,000 Jews, almost 4,000 of whom were children, were crowded together at once in the Vélodrome d'Hiver sports arena. Space was scarce and circumstances were appalling, with no arrangements for food, water, or sanitary facilities. The glass ceiling made the heat in the Vélodrome unbearable. After five days, Jews incarcerated at the Vélodrome d'Hiver were transferred to other transit camps outside Paris. At the end of July, the remaining adults were separated from their children and deported to Auschwitz. Over 3,000 children remained interned, orphaned, until they were deported to Auschwitz as well.

The Vélodrome d'Hiver roundup was organized by René Bousquet, secretary general of the French national police; Louis Darquier de Pellepoix, Commissioner for Jewish Affairs under the Vichy Regime; SS-Hauptsturmführer Theodor Dannecker, head of Adolf Eichmann's Judenreferat (Jewish Section) in France; and SS-Obersturmführer Helmut Knochen, head of the German Security Police in France. It was a coordinated effort between the Germans and the French to eradicate the immigrant Jews, and the French willingly collaborated. In order to guarantee the participation of the French police in the roundups, Nazi officials agreed to focus on foreign and stateless Jews, thus initially sparing the native French Jewish population from deportation. The Jews who were part of the roundup were not limited to those living in and around Paris. The dragnet extended to the south, even as far as Lot-et-Garonne.

This was the danger from which we were being shielded at summer camp.

After the other kids departed summer camp, leaving us with only a handful of children, I developed a tremendous fear, sadness, doubt, insecurity—whatever you may call it. The worst part was that I could not understand how my parents, who loved us, who were such good parents, so devoted, so caring, would suddenly not want us to come home. How could this be possible?

A number of other Jewish boys remained in camp past September, which was when I thought we would surely leave. But, as September came and went, I realized that we were not going back to Saint-Pardoux and into the arms of our parents. Whatever the camp director or staff told us was obviously to comfort us, but they were unable to allay my increasing anxiety and feelings of abandonment. Two weeks had turned into two months—and two months seemed like an eternity for a boy of eight.

During this period, I became a bed wetter. This happened frequently. We lived in a dormitory, each of us with our own bed. It was a long dormitory, with beds lined up on both sides of the room. The other children didn't have this problem. They made fun of me, saying that my bed stank. Then I would have to change my linens and go back to bed in wet pajamas or whatever clothes I was wearing when I first fell asleep. I was embarrassed and miserable.

My brother did not share this manifestation of anxiety. He was so young that he didn't understand that there was anything unusual about our being kept at camp. To go to a summer camp to have fun with other kids was understandable, but when those other kids went home and we and just a few other boys stayed, that was incomprehensible to me. I could not fathom why our parents didn't want us, why they insisted that we stay there.

I was told by Monsieur Cohn—as gently and compassionately as possible—that I was now responsible for Herbert. I took that responsibility seriously. He was, in that moment, my only family. We were alone together, yet we were totally dependent on others for our survival, our food, our lodging, for everything that would normally have been provided by our parents. We were wards of the Jewish community. Meanwhile, it felt as if our parents had abandoned us, despite what the director told us. In my mind, we were orphans along with the other children who, like us, had been placed in the arms of strangers.

I remember celebrating Sukkoth, the Jewish holiday of the harvest, which takes place in the early fall. By that time, we were supposed to have been back home. And yet, there we were, still at camp. The weeklong holiday is observed by building and spending time in a sukkah, a temporary outdoor structure that is a representation of the harvest season. The inside of the sukkah, which is made with branches, is decorated with fruits and vegetables that are hung as symbols of the harvest. Along with dwelling in the sukkah, we lift and shake the *lulav* (a bundle of fronds from four plant species that include a palm branch, three branches of myrtle, and two willow branches) with an *etrog* (a fragrant, yellow or green bumpy citrus fruit). Sukkoth takes place after the celebration of the New Year, Rosh Hashanah, and Yom Kippur, the Day of Atonement, the holiest day in the Jewish calendar.

The camp staff built a sukkah on the balcony of a building on the second floor. It was wonderful. It smelled delicious from the pine and the other freshly cut tree branches, and the counselors added lights and some colored paper to make it festive—and it was! And, of course, it had a roof, made of branches and palms, and we ate all our meals there during the week of Sukkoth.

Looking back, this was the staff's effort not just to teach us about our faith, but also to cheer us up in our depression.

One day, some people came to the camp. I have an impression of a woman and some men, who I would later learn were representatives of a Quaker organization tasked with getting Jewish children out of France to safety. They came to inspect us and to determine who might be selected to go by ship to England or even to the United States.

The Quakers had formed an aid organization called the American Friends Service Committee, which was active in the south of France as early as 1939. By late summer 1942, when we were still at summer camp, the Quakers began the painful process of selecting children who would be given visas and transportation to leave France. They hoped that as many as 1,000 children might leave, but they were able to arrange for the "liberation" of 250 who crossed into Spain and left by boat from Lisbon, Portugal. By November 1942, the Americans had attacked German strongholds in northern Africa, and the border between France and Spain was closed. All the American Quakers were ordered to leave, despite the fact that they were an aid agency and of no threat to the Germans. Some of the workers defied these orders and ended up in concentration camps.

I remember standing in line waiting my turn to be interviewed by a well-dressed Quaker woman. All of us were scared that we would make a mistake when we were interviewed. The interviewers were very motherly toward us and spoke in gentle tones so as not to scare us.

"What is your name?" my interviewer asked.

I hesitated for a moment, since just weeks earlier my name had been changed from Alfred Lakritz to Alfred LaCroix. I summoned my courage and answered, "My name is Alfred LaCroix, and my brother is Herbert LaCroix."

The woman asked, "Have you been vaccinated?" Without proper vaccinations, children were not permitted to travel outside France. I don't remember how I answered this question or whether we had been vaccinated in Germany or Belgium before we arrived in France.

For whatever reason, we were not chosen by the Quakers to leave France, or the doors to England and the United States were closed to us due to sudden changes in government policies.

And so we remained in France to face the horrific dangers of World War II and the Nazi campaign to eradicate all people whose only crime was to have been born a Jew. Here is the directive from Heinrich Himmler made public at the Wannsee Conference articulating the Final Solution:

I herewith order that the resettlement of the entire Jewish population of the Government-General be carried out and completed by December 31, 1942. From December 31, 1942, no persons of Jewish origin may remain within the Government-General, unless they are in collection camps in Warsaw, Cracow, Czestochowa, Radom, and Lublin. All other work on which Jewish labor is employed must be finished by that date, or, in the event that this is not possible, it must be transferred to one of the collection camps.

These measures are required with a view to the necessary ethnic division of races and peoples for the New Order in Europe, and also in the interests of the security and cleanliness of the German Reich and its sphere of interest. Every breach of this regulation spells a danger to quiet and order in the entire German sphere of interest, a point of application for the resistance movement and a source of moral and physical pestilence.For all these reasons a total cleansing is necessary and therefore to be carried out. Cases in which the date set cannot be observed will be reported to me in time, so that I can see to corrective action at an early date. All requests by other offices for changes or permits for exceptions to be made must be presented to me personally.

Heil Hitler!

Heinrich Himmler[8]

---

[8] https://www.yadvashem.org/docs/himmler-order-for-completion-of-final-solution.html

CHAPTER 7

Let Our Fate Be a Warning to You

On August 26, 1942, six weeks after the Vélodrome d'Hiver roundup in Paris, the Vichy regime arrested some 6,000 Jews in unoccupied zones, including Lot-et-Garonne.

There were no German military stationed in Lot-et-Garonne. All the arrests were carried out entirely by the local French police. They had lists of names, and they had people's addresses. The authorities would turn up at people's homes and say, "Open up—police!" The police targeted all foreign or stateless Jews, including refugees who had fled from Belgium.[9]

My parents were on that list, probably because they were active in the underground Jewish resistance movement and were being spied upon by neighbors unsympathetic to their plight. On that August morning, at 5 a.m., they were dragged from their bed and arrested along with other immigrant Jews.

[9] https://www.france24.com/en/france/20220826-vichy-s-biggest-stain-the-august-1942-roundup-80-years-on

They were transported to the grand ballroom of the only hotel in Marmande. It turned out that essentially all the refugee Jews in the area had been arrested in the same manner.

I suspect that many of the police officers involved in this roundup had misgivings. There were police who were kind and helpful to Jews. Some even participated in the French Resistance, and they often alerted Jews to potential threats at great peril to themselves, risking not only their jobs but their lives. But in light of a direct order from Paris and the complicity of many other officers, there was only so much that the good police officers could have done. Disobeying orders would be perilous.

Reichsführer-SS Heinrich Himmler—one of the most powerful men in Nazi Germany and the demon considered to be the architect of the Holocaust—set a goal of the deportation of 100,000 Jews from France to extermination camps "in order to completely liberate the regions of all foreign Jews." For whatever reason, that number was reduced to 40,000 soon after.

My parents and other Jews were moved from the hotel in Marmande and forced to board a train where they were locked into cattle cars. There was no food, no windows, and no bathrooms—only a bucket was provided for this purpose. Using it was humiliating, but what choice did they have? They were taken to a detention camp established by the French in Casseneuil in the Lot-et-Garonne region in southwest France, twenty-seven kilometers from the principal town of Agen. The camp was dirty and rudimentary. I wonder what the residents of the area thought about having a detention camp in their midst. Did they understand what was happening and where these people were being sent and why? Or did they simply put their heads down, hoping that they would stay out of trouble themselves?

My mother learned that the French had created some loopholes to incarceration at the Casseneuil camp, some exceptions to turning over Jews who had been arrested in a grand sweep. One of the exceptions was that if a woman was pregnant, she would be exempt. (Perhaps my mother had learned this from other members of the Resistance whom she and my father worked with prior to their arrest.)

My mother cleverly and bravely told the authorities that she was pregnant. She was taken to the infirmary where she was examined, revealing that she was lying out of desperation. A military doctor at Casseneuil asked her whether she had other children, and she replied, "Yes, I have two boys and I want them to live."

The doctor understood, and out of sympathy for my mother's situation, he declared that she was pregnant. The nurse attending the doctor (a Catholic nun) also prepared the notes and nodded at my mother. The authorities, who may or may not have personally hated Jews, abided by the doctor's diagnosis and allowed my parents to return home. The doctor and nurse saved my parents' lives. My mother never mentioned the doctor's name, if she ever knew it, but her description suggests that it might have been a famously benevolent doctor by the name of Griffier, who was known to have worked at another internment camp named Gurs. According to the historian Marie Juliette Vieleazat Petitcol, several other detainees owed their lives to Dr. Griffier.

What a stroke of luck that my mother had this information regarding the exemption of pregnancy, and that the doctor took pity on her. It's amazing that they let my father go as well.

My mother and father returned to Saint-Pardoux, cautiously and fearfully carrying on with life, including praying, observing the Sabbath, and meeting in makeshift spaces for rituals. For whatever reason, the French authorities were not interested in Jews' religious lives. Perhaps the Nazis wanted Jews to feel comfortable being out in the open, so they would be easier to identify and abduct.

My parents continued to work for several families, including the Ros family. Pierre and Jeanne Ros were Catholics who had escaped Italy under Mussolini. My mother made herself useful by performing many odds jobs in town in addition to her work as a seamstress. She made friends and was well liked among both Christians and immigrant Jews. My father worked in the fields and tried to avoid being seen as much as possible.

My parents also stayed involved in the French Resistance despite the danger. It is possible that some of the police knew of their association and passed on information to them despite their orders to the contrary. These were police whose conscience did not allow them to remain silent despite the risk to their own lives.

* * *

In February 1943, over eight months since Herbert and I had left for summer camp, the police knocked on my parents' door in Saint-Pardoux for the second time.

My mother screamed, cried, and demanded that they not take her husband. Screaming back, the French police manhandled, beat, and took my father to the police station in Marmande. No one would tell my father what was happening or why it was happening.

My father's arrest was not part of an indiscriminate mass roundup of refugee Jews, as the first one had been. This time, the French authorities targeted him personally. He was known by the police to be the leader of the Jewish resistance. They left my mother behind this time. Had she been taken with him, she might have met the same horrific fate as he did. I cannot imagine the panic she felt, fearing that perhaps my father would not come back. Word was spreading that the German attacks against the Jews was escalating, and that their ultimate goal was to accomplish *judenrein*—the complete obliteration of the Jews from the face of the earth—and the sooner, the better.

My father was taken first to Gurs. Just across from the Spanish border in the extreme southwestern corner of France, the Gurs camp had been founded in 1939 to house people fleeing from the Franco regime in Spain. When the Vichy government took over in 1940, it was converted into a detention center for Jews and other people whom the Nazis considered "undesirable." The camp was rudimentary, and its most distinctive feature was its constantly muddy ground due to frequent rainstorms and bad drainage. In total, 65,000 people were interned at Gurs during the war until it was decommissioned in 1945. One in four of the deportees died in Gurs or other French camps, 11 percent succeeded in emigrating overseas, 12 percent hid out in France, and 40 percent (around 2,600 deportees) were transported to Auschwitz after July 1942. The fate of the remaining 600 deportees is unknown. Due to the filthy conditions in the camp, many detained there died of diseases even before they were transported elsewhere to face their fate.

My father was kept in this camp for several days. Then he was forced into a cattle train, with one hundred prisoners crammed in one car with no windows, no fresh air, no food, and no toilet, except one pot each for men and women. They traveled for many hours, unaware that they were heading north into a German-occupied zone near Paris.

The train took my father and the other prisoners to a camp called Drancy, which was in a northeast suburb of Paris. Drancy was a housing project that had been appropriated by the French police on behalf of the Nazis in 1942 for the detainment and deportation of Jews in France. My father was one of 64,000 people—mostly Jews—who passed through Drancy during the war. Only 2,000 of them survived. Drancy later became known as France's major camp for the detention of Jews arrested throughout the country. Imagine all these horrors taking place in close proximity to the Eiffel Tower, the Arc de Triomphe, and France's most important cathedral, Notre-Dame. Surely French citizens were aware of what was happening in Drancy, but they did nothing to mobilize its liberation. Instead, they cowered in their apartments, their *maisons particuliers*, their cafés, their universities, hoping that they would avoid a similar fate.

There was a set of four-story buildings in Drancy that were unfinished, without windows, sanitary facilities, or furniture, served by a dozen or so stairs. The living conditions were terrifying, with as many as 7,000 prisoners living there at any one time. Crammed in groups of seventy in foul-smelling chambers meant for fifty, internees were forced to lie down on hard concrete floors. There were no cots or mattresses, and there was practically nothing to eat. The last hours in Drancy before they were transported elsewhere were atrocious. All persons were searched and stripped of any jewels or money that they had managed to hide. They were forbidden to leave their quarters and used buckets on the stairways as toilets, which quickly became full.

In Drancy, my father was allowed to send a postcard to his wife, and hopefully to us, his children, whom he had not seen since June 1942 and about whose whereabouts he could not be certain. It is one of those messages that carries the feeling of the writer not just in the words, but in the manner in which it is written. The note reads:

> My dearest wife and dearest Alfred and Herbert, I am letting you know that I am in good health, and as of today I find myself in the Drancy Camp. Tonight I leave [illegible]. Compliments and kisses. Have <u>courage</u>. Do not forget [illegible] your husband and father Simche Lakritz.

The word "courage" was underlined by my father. His message ends with the misspelled word "Adjeu" and is dated March 3, 1943.

In the French language, *adieu* means "goodbye." It does not mean "farewell," "see you soon," or "until next time." It does not carry the casual connotations of *au revoir* or the breeziness of *bonne nuit*. It is "goodbye." *Adieu* means finality.

The word directed to his children and to his wife is *courage*, meaning the same in French as it does in English. "Courage" is a big word. It conveys hope. Hope that there may be a better day ahead.

If you unite the two—*courage* and *adieu*—the message from my father to his sons and to his wife could be interpreted as follows: "I am going to die. I am going to die a horrible death at this young age. But for you, I pray that there is hope. Maybe I am a lamb. Maybe I am among the sacrificed. Be courageous, my loved ones."

My father was just thirty-five years old.

Of course, my father did not know the scope of the Nazi plan. He did not know that he was one of six million Jews who would ultimately be killed by the time the war ended in 1945. He did not know of the enormity of the crimes of the Nazis and their willing accomplices. He knew only of those prisoners with whom he rubbed shoulders who, like him, were herded into cattle cars to an unknown destination.

According to his Certificate of Disappearance, my father left Drancy on March 4, 1943, in Convoy Number 50 bound for Poland, a day after he mailed his final postcard to my mother, my brother, and me.

My father was transported to Auschwitz, in German-occupied Poland. There, the Nazis had established a concentration camp, built in part with assistance from the Poles. Auschwitz was a killing place where people were sorted, some for immediate gassing and death, while others were selected for labor, human experiments, and tasks demanded by the Germans. The Auschwitz concentration camp is remembered for the wrought iron German sign at the gates that greeted prisoners as they were unloaded off the trucks and separated into "useful" and "useless" groups: *Arbeit macht frei* ("Work sets you free"). What it came to mean is: work will keep you alive here until you are too sick, too famished, too tired, too broken down to lift a shovel or work on an assembly line, and then we will get rid of you.

In the three years he spent in France, my father had developed many skills and grown far stronger than he would have been had he remained behind a desk in Kiel managing the finances or organizing employees at his father's business. Because he was still young and healthy, my father was transported from Auschwitz to another camp called Majdanek, south of Warsaw, where he was selected for hard labor.

The camp was nicknamed Majdanek ("Little Majdan") in 1941 by local residents, as it was adjacent to the Lublin ghetto of

Majdan Tatarski. Nazi documents initially described the site as a prisoner-of-war camp of the Waffen-SS based on how it was funded and operated. It was renamed by the Reich Security Main Office as Konzentrationslager Lublin on April 9, 1943, but the local Polish name remained more popular.

It was located in the Lublin District of the *Generalgouvernement*—the government of Nazi-occupied Poland. This district included parts of what is now Ukraine, including the city of Lvov (L'viv). In other words, my father had been sent back to his homeland: Galicia. But this time he was there as a prisoner, not as a Jew fleeing Russian troops.

The camp was visible from the city of Lublin, just a few kilometers away on the main road where city residents went to and from work each day and to the farms in the outlying areas.

Majdanek was one of the worst of all the concentration camps (although is there a hierarchy of horror and torture? Perhaps not.). Auschwitz probably killed more prisoners, but Majdanek killed them in the most horrific ways. It was part of the Nazi network of death factories, designed to wipe the Jews off the face of the earth, in efficient and swift means with the least drain on important resources that were used to fight the war. It was part of the Nazi campaign of *judenrein*—cleansing the earth of all Jews. (This is different from *judenfrei* which means freeing the earth of all Jews.) The Nazi tentacles extended as far away as Japan and Shanghai, where Nazi officials targeted Jews and put them in ghettos with the help of local Chinese citizens who were trying to escape imprisonment themselves. It is almost unimaginable how the Germans were able to cover so much ground while fighting a war at the same time. It could only have been accomplished by people who collaborated with the Nazis, believing that the Jews should not live under any circumstances, and what they left behind could be gathered up and redistributed to those people who lacked money and resources. Gold fillings, shoes, clothing, jewelry hidden in clothing, wire-rimmed glasses, even hair—everything taken from the Jews had a purpose. Even their bodies could be used as fertilizer or fuel.

Prisoners in Majdanek were given only enough food to keep them standing on their feet to work. Their labor included breaking up stones and assembling machinery for the war effort. They wore the thinnest of pajama-type clothing and slept in bunks stacked three high with no room to move around. Little by little, most prisoners died of starvation and disease. Other prisoners' skeleton-like bodies were asphyxiated in gas chambers. The Nazis didn't care if they lost laborers. They had many other prisoners whom they could move from one camp to another to keep the operation going. And the Nazis intended to kill all the prisoners once they lost their usefulness.

Majdanek was not originally intended to be an extermination camp. It was built, starting October 1, 1941 (the same date when construction on Auschwitz-Birkenau began, under the same order from Berlin) as a labor camp, with inmates working at a nearby Steyr-Daimler-Puch weapons factory. The camp housed not only Jews but also thousands of Russian prisoners of war, many of whom were captured in the Battle of Kiev, which lasted from July to September 1942. The camp's capacity at its peak was around 50,000, with 227 structures in total, making it one of the largest concentration camps.

Six months after its opening, Majdanek was outfitted with the infrastructure of extermination: gas chambers. Eventually, Majdanek had seven. They took their first victims in September

1942. Majdanek famously operated its gas chambers in plain sight. Inmates entered but did not exit, and other inmates could clearly see what was happening. This is how casual the Nazis' approach to killing had become. Over 300,000 inmates passed through Majdanek.

In a symbol of the supreme perversity of the Nazi regime, the commandant of Majdanek was the washed-up Schutzstaffel (SS) officer Karl Otto Koch. He had previously run several other concentration camps, dating back to 1936 when Heinrich Himmler established the first camps for undesirables and political opponents of the Nazis. In his previous appointment, in charge of Buchenwald, he had been accused of corruption, fraud, embezzlement, drunkenness, sexual offenses, and a murder. For this, Koch, who held the rank of Standartenführer, was "rewarded" with another command post, this time at Majdanek. His incompetence led to the escape of eighty-six Soviet prisoners of war in August 1942, after which he was relieved of his command. Toward the end of the war, Koch was convicted of embezzlement and executed by a firing squad.

Koch's successor was similarly corrupt. Arthur Hermann Florstedt took command in October 1942. When German authorities discovered that he had been stealing valuables—including gold, furs, and jewelry—that had been stripped from the camp's Jewish inmates, he was convicted and also executed.

Throughout the summer and fall of 1943, when my father was a prisoner in Majdanek, uprisings took place at several concentration camps in Poland. Prisoners rebelled, killed guards, and escaped. These uprisings made the Nazis, and in particular Heinrich Himmler, nervous. He wanted to quell these uprisings in the most direct way possible—death. I have no record of my father participating in one of these uprisings, but knowing the kind of person he was and how courageous he was, I suspect that he might have participated in planning one such uprising, or even might have tried to escape.

On November 3, 1943, eight months after my father was transported from Drancy, the German authorities sent in more than 150 Gestapo officers clad in their black uniforms decorated with the skull and bones and carrying machine guns to Majdanek and its satellite camps. A loudspeaker ordered the inmates to exit their barracks and to follow the instructions of their commanding concentration camp soldiers and assistants. They were ordered to create three ditches of a dimension that they could not possibly comprehend. Of course, some of them had to jump in as the ditches got deeper and deeper.

At some point the Germans said it was enough; then some of these internees were ordered to start picking up and transporting bodies of internees who had died of starvation and diseases and dump them into the ditch. When that task was done, all the Jewish internees who had labored in this matter were ordered to strip. Their clothing was dirty from digging and carrying dead bodies covered in excrement, vomit, blood, and piss. Perhaps the prisoners thought, or hoped against hope, that they were going to be handed clean prison garb.

They were ordered to stand at attention in front of and alongside the big ditches they had excavated and that already had many bodies lying in them. Then they were ordered by the officers to turn around, to look at what they had done. There was no disobeying of orders. There was no purpose, and no means to disobey. The order was an absolute order, because they were watched by guards standing alongside them or surveying them from towers, all of whom carried machine guns. When they turned around, the Nazi soldiers shot all the men, most falling directly into the pit they had been digging for hours, on top of the bodies of those prisoners already lying at the bottom of the ditch.

This mass execution operation began at six or seven in the morning on November 3 and lasted all day until five o'clock. The killings continued over the course of three days across Majdanek, Trawniki, and Poniatowa, a massacre of a minimum of 42,000 Jews. Over 18,000 human souls were killed at Majdanek. This slaughter has an infamous name in German: *Aktion "Erntefest"* (Operation "Harvest Festival"). Music played over loudspeakers at both Majdanek and Trawniki to drown out the noise of the mass shootings so that the townspeople would not hear what was going on. But many knew what was happening and did nothing to stop it—or had no way to stop it.

The killings at Majdanek were the largest single German-perpetrated massacre at any concentration camp during the Holocaust. The camp remained in operation until it was liberated by the Soviet army at the end of July 1944. After visiting the Soviet-occupied camp shortly after its liberation, William H. Lawrence, a reporter for The *New York Times*, opened his article on Majdanek with the words: "I have just seen the most terrible place on the face of the earth."

My father was one of the prisoners murdered during the Harvest Festival.

All the bodies that were thrown into the ditches in Majdanek were cremated, and their ashes were scattered under leaves or buried out of sight. After the war and the liberation of the camp, piles of ashes were eventually recovered and placed in an enormous mausoleum and memorial to the dead that was constructed years later in 1969. It sits on a path to the crematorium with its seven gas chambers. The mausoleum is dome-shaped and pockmarked, as if it had been hit by a bomb. On its top inscribed in Polish are the words: "Let our fate be a warning to you."

Perhaps my father's ashes are among those in this mausoleum. I have never been there. I am not sure I have the courage to stand there. I would much rather think of my father alive, vibrant, and loving. But if I were there I would surely daven while reciting the Mourner's Kaddish, which begins: "Exalted and hallowed be His great Name. Throughout the world which He has created according to His Will. May He establish His kingship, bring forth His redemption and hasten the coming of His Redeemer…" And then I might look up into an overcast sky to see a hawk circling overhead, casting a shadow onto the spot where my father had lifted a sledgehammer to break up a boulder and then, as a commandant screamed the order, lifted a shovel to dig the ditch that became his grave.

I have a photograph of my mother during the period after my father was carted away—hoping against hope that by some miracle her beloved husband would be saved. In the photograph she is sitting at a table outside the barn which served as her home in Saint-Pardoux. On the table is her sewing machine and a framed photograph of Herbert and me wearing clothing given to us by OSE—sabots and berets. The photograph must have been given to her by a representative of the aid organization. If you look into her eyes, you can see such sadness, such loneliness, such pain, such agony, for fear she has lost her children and her husband.

For years, I did not know how or where my father died. My mother and I did not talk about it. But many years later after I established my law practice, I began to do research about my father and other family members. I owed it to them. And it was during that long period that I read about Majdanek and learned what happened there and how my father must have been tortured and killed. I discovered his name and his place of birth and death on page 1,550 of the *Gedenkbuch*.

I do not know if I am any better off now than I was when I was ignorant of these facts, but I needed to know what happened to my father, no matter how horrible his fate. In some ways it has helped me put some closure to his story.

At some point, my mother showed me the postcard my father had written. I held it in my hands. I read his goodbye, and I thought about whether I had summoned the courage that he wished for me. "*Adieu*," I whispered to him.

The time between my father's arrest and his murder was eight months. That he survived that long speaks not only to his physical strength but to his will to survive despite all the torture that was meted out to him. If only he could have found a means of escape—but that was not to be. He left behind a loving wife and two sons, Herb and me. I spent the rest of my life without the father whom I admired and looked up to—a religious man, a man of great intelligence, a brave soul. I sometimes wonder if his spiritual beliefs held him up from one day to the next, whether he organized secret prayer groups at Majdanek and encouraged others to remain positive in the hope that a miracle would happen and they would be saved.

* * *

Monsieur Gérard Guillot, the former Secrétaire du Mairie of Marmande, considers himself responsible for my father's arrest and murder. He admitted to me years later when I visited Marmande: "There is nothing the authorities can do to me now because I am too old and sick, but I could have saved your father. When they ordered your father's arrest, I did not realize that the Marmande chief of police was also sympathetic to his plight. We were both of the same mind. Had I been aware of that in 1943, we could have done something together, but at the time I was afraid he would oppose me, so I remained silent."

I was shocked and horrified to hear this, but he had a crisis of conscience and went about saving others and helping my mother during the remaining war years. Monsieur Guillot made sure that my mother received a pension from the French government as the wife of a war hero. He secured a place for her to live in Marmande. He showed my mother great kindness, and his son became my brother's good friend. In my opinion, Gérard Guillot should have been named to the Righteous Among the Nations in Yad Vashem, a list of Gentiles who risked their lives to save Jews during the Holocaust. When I did my research, I could not find his name among the Righteous. Perhaps I have misspelled it, or perhaps he was overlooked by those historians compiling the list.

Monsieur Guillot embodied both evil and good—timidity and courage. He tried his best to make up for his transgressions, and I have forgiven him in light of his many acts of kindness toward my mother and others.

As for the people who killed my father, willingly and deliberately, I cannot forget and I cannot forgive.

I often ask myself, When do you decide to cross the line between right and wrong? Where does one learn to mistreat another human being? I do not have the answer but in my lifetime I have seen the best and the worst of humanity.

The postcard my father Simche Lakritz sent on March 3, 1943, before being transported from Drancy to Auschwitz to Majdanek. He instructs us to have courage, and wishes us adieu.

Smoke rising from Majdanek, 1943.

Jews marching to their death on "bloody Wednesday," November 3, 1943.

The burial monument at Majdanek where the ashes of the dead were collected
and interred in 1969. On the stone are carved words in Polish,
"Let our fate be a warning to you."

CHAPTER 8

Evading the Nazis

If my father's letter to the camp director instructing him to keep his sons had been lost in the mail, which functioned sporadically, or if my parents had not made the decision to keep us in summer camp, we might eventually have been sent to Drancy, to Auschwitz, and to our deaths. Instead, we survived. Our parents and many other parents sent their children into "the arms of strangers" organized by the OSE to protect their children, to hide them, to feed them, to clothe them, to do whatever they could to make sure they were out of the reach of the enemy.

My father sent four other letters, which were saved by my great-uncle Max Fass in Oakland and later given to my mother, who passed them on to me. My father wrote what he knew about what was happening to my brother and me, and he noted that he was sending fifty francs for our care at the summer camp. When I look at my father's handwriting, I try to imagine how he must have felt and whether he held out hope for his future and that of his wife and children.

After we left summer camp following Sukkoth, we headed for one relatively safe French town after another—but they were safe for only a short time. The Nazis were always on our trail. I sometimes wonder what they wanted from us. We weren't strong enough to do manual labor to help the Nazis in the war effort. It must have been that they just wanted to get rid of us—to annihilate the next generation of Jews.

So, we went into hiding.

Château de Chabannes in Creuse

We remained in the summer camp in the care of Monsieur le Directeur Cohn and other volunteers until mid-October 1942. Then, without explanation, we were moved to another place in the middle of France until it, too, was no longer safe. Of course, we did not know it at the time, but the authorities might have learned of our whereabouts, and it was no longer safe.

The OSE had a fully functioning false documentation service which operated throughout the war years. They gave us false birth certificates with the name "LaCroix." All of a sudden, my brother and I were Alfred and Herbert LaCroix, which means "cross" in French. The OSE determined that the name Lakritz might have signaled to the Nazis that we were Jewish children, and it was not safe to carry that name. So once again my name was changed. I had to practice this name so that I would not make a mistake, and I helped Herbert do the same. A child's name and the way to spell it is one of the first things a child learns, and now we had to adjust to another name, learn to spell it, and say it with ease so that we wouldn't be suspected of lying. I don't know how many other children were given a new name and a new identification card.

We were also given a food card with the name LaCroix on it so that when food was distributed, we would be eligible to receive it. As the war escalated, food became scarcer, even in the south of France, because crops were reserved to feed the German army and the Vichy officials.

The OSE operated primarily with donations from the United States. The money was collected from generous Jews who had some understanding of the plight of children like Herbert and me. What they would learn about the atrocities of the Nazis leaked out slowly, and the news was so horrific as to be difficult to believe. And the media was slow to disseminate what they knew. In fact, *The New York Times* was owned by a Jewish family, the Sulzbergers, who allegedly wanted to eschew the label of being a "Jewish newspaper" and therefore sometimes downplayed coverage by keeping stories of atrocities against the Jews off the front page.

The place Herbert and I stayed once we were moved from summer camp was located in the village of Chabannes, a hamlet in the Creuse region, a remote, beautiful, and unspoiled area of central France. The people of the village had a strong spirit of independence, freedom, and justice carried over from the early days of the French Republic and reinforced by the precepts of Freemasonry. Geographically and politically, the village was the ideal location for the Œuvre de Secours aux Enfants.

The rallying cry of the OSE, a Jewish organization, was: "We must save the children."

While our residence was described as a château, it was actually a private home owned by two Christian sisters, Irene and Renée Paillasou, who were teachers. One of them was married to Félix Chevrier, a Freemason and courageous journalist. It was he who directed the operation of the château, which became a temporary home for Jewish children who ranged in age from two to seventeen.[10] Rachel Levin Pludermacher was the first teacher recruited by the OSE to instruct Jewish refugee children, and Georges Loinger, also of the OSE, forsook his engineering career to teach children gymnastics so that they would be fit and could run for their lives if necessary. Some of these individuals participated in the documentary *The Children of Chabannes* and helped to explain on camera how at least 250,000 Jews managed to survive the war in Vichy, France, while 76,000 were sent to their deaths. These may seem like numbers to the reader, but my brother and I were two of the 250,000 who survived due to the bravery of these kind souls.

The château where we were hidden had the usual array of games, but there was only so much to do. We had no toys, no books. We were given strings to play with, and we played cat's cradle, where you put the string between the fingers of both hands. All of us got good at that game. We played pick-up sticks. Our caregivers took us for walks in the countryside.

We sometimes played a game to search for four-leaf clovers. The staff had us do this, figuring, correctly, that it would keep us busy. Sometimes a child would pluck a leaf off one sprig of clover and try to attach it to another to claim that it had four leaves. I don't think that ruse ever worked, but we must have been curious to see if our caregivers could be fooled. And as I look back on this game, I realize that it was a way to keep our hopes up—that by some magic, a four-leaf clover would appear, or that we could make one. For anyone who has lived through a tragedy, hope is

---

[10] https://www.yadvashem.org/yv/en/exhibitions/childrens-homes/chabannes/index.asp

what keeps a person alive, even in the darkest of times. Hope that someone will be alive, hope that a child will find a four-leaf clover.

Herbert and I were outfitted with clothes and shoes. Remember, we were growing boys and the shoes we wore when we boarded the train for camp no longer fit. Instead, we were given sabots, which are similar to wooden shoes made in Holland, and we wore berets on our heads. Someone took a picture of Herbert and me in our donated attire.

The food we ate consisted mainly of turnips and potatoes; once a week we had a small piece of beef, and the bread was made partially with wheat, partially with sawdust that we had to pick out. At night some of the older boys would go on forays to steal vegetables from the neighboring farms. If a farmer saw a gang of boys running across the field, they would shoot BB guns, but as far as I knew no one was injured.

From time to time the French police would arrive unannounced at the chateau and take away one or more of the older boys. Sometimes they would be returned, sometimes not.

The two sisters who owned the château showered us with love and affection and took wonderful care of us, although nothing could replace the love of my parents. I remember we were scheduled to leave Chabannes because we were being looked for by the Vichy authorities. One of the sisters—I must admit—had a special feeling for me. She wanted to give me something to remember her by and as a protective token. She gave me a postcard with a picture of Noah and his ark.

I asked her why we had to leave Chabannes.

She said, "Tomorrow we don't know what is going to happen." Her answer was vague because she did not want to scare me, but when I looked into her eyes, I knew that we were in danger. And when I studied the postcard, I understood its message—that God wanted to protect us.

Members of the OSE took us to a railroad station, and we boarded a train in the middle of the night with chaperones, leaving behind Félix Chevrier and Irene and Renée Paillassou, who were all honored years later by Yad Vashem as "Righteous Among the Nations." Herbert and I were beneficiaries of their collective goodness and selflessness in the face of evil.

Évian-les-Bains, Haute-Savoie

From Chabannes we traveled southeast to a mountaintop at the edge of Lac Léman in the beautiful town of Évian-les-Bains in the Haute-Savoie region, about an hour from Geneva and across the lake from Lausanne, Switzerland. (Ironically, this was a spa town where there was a large international conference a few years earlier instituting the policy of stamping a big red letter *J* on the passports of Jews. The conference was intended to solve the refugee problem, but its major accomplishment was to set up subcommittees, and spend money on hotel rooms and delicious food for the representatives of thirty-two nations and NGO observers.)

Other children from our group were taken to the Pyrenees and ended up in Spain. We had a chance to go to Italy because many Italians were sympathetic, but it was deemed too dangerous because Mussolini was aligned with Hitler, and who knew what he might do to Jewish children. It was a gamble that our custodians weren't willing to take.

While we stayed in Évian we were portrayed to the local townspeople as French orphan children. That was the best excuse for why we were there.

During our time in Évian I was registered to go to school. I was fluent in French by then, so I became Alfred LaCroix, a Catholic French boy from Saint-Pardoux-du-Breuil who didn't speak German; my outside identity was partially altered, and I strained to remember not to give my real identity away.

My memories of our periods of hiding with other children in Évian include hikes into the mountains with the breathtaking sights of the Alps—snowcapped mountains and glaciers including Mont Blanc in Chamonix, which was about seventy kilometers away but so large that it could be seen from where we stayed. The terrain was full of vegetation and trees, including beautiful red, yellow and gold-colored poppies that remind me of the paintings of Pierre-Auguste Renoir. When I would look down and across Lac Léman, I could see Geneva, Switzerland. I could see freedom and escape from the pursuit and the hunt. I saw safety. But apparently the road to that safety was barred to us by the Swiss government that, because of Switzerland's neutral status, had closed its borders to any French refugees who were trying to escape the Germans—at least, this was their official position. Maybe a few Jews were hidden in Switzerland, but I have no knowledge of this, and I never heard any of our custodians considering the idea of sneaking us into Switzerland at any point.

There were older children and some a little younger than my brother and me who lived with us. I don't remember their names. When I look at the photograph I have of that time and of our group of children, I still remember many of their features very vividly. I remember one girl who was older than me by several years. She must have been nice to me, since I was one of the younger boys, and I probably allowed her to express her motherly instincts. I don't remember other boys being mean to me, nor do

I remember engaging in meanness toward anyone else. As anxious as I was, I had gotten over bed-wetting by that time. I was assigned to look out for a boy who was afraid of getting lost on hikes, so I used to take care of him. I was bigger and older than he was. It was a lot of responsibility because I also had to look out for my brother. I promised my parents I would do so, and in my mind I would be failing my parents if he left my sight even for more than a few minutes. Again, this was but another burden that I carried with me, and that must have strained my nerves, even when I was not aware of it. Over time, the accumulations of these stresses and strains must have shaped my personality and instilled in me childhood trauma that I have carried into my adulthood.

On the second floor of the chalet in Évian we had dormitories and playrooms. Downstairs and outside the building there was a play area. I remember that we were allowed to go to school there by walking down the street and turning right. In the same general direction there was also a gray stone church.

We stayed in Évian during the fall and early winter of 1943. I remember that it was a time when chestnuts (*marrons*) were plentiful. The chestnuts reminded me of Antwerp before we escaped to France. Vendors sold them from carts and wrapped them in newspaper. It was true in France, too. What a wonderful thing it was if you had a little money and you could buy one of those horns with chestnuts—warm, hot, delicious chestnuts off a grill. But I didn't have money. With envy and hunger, I would look and watch others being able to buy and eat these chestnuts. The air was filled with the delicious smell.

We played games with rudimentary toys (such as strings) and were led on hikes climbing some of the mountains and observing the wonderful, marvelous sights of the Alps. We sang French marching songs. I remember one in particular, "Le Chanson de l'oignon," which dates back to the time of Napoleon. The song tells the soldiers: *"Au pas comrades!"* ("Step along, comrades!")

I am sure it was in Évian where I learned to appreciate nature and acquired my love of hiking. It was both a source of exercise and pleasure. It was relatively safe, and it didn't cost anything. I have carried my love of hiking and the outdoors into my adulthood and enjoy nature to this day, not only being in it, but painting it through my artistic endeavors. What amazes me is that we had so many pleasant times despite the hostile circumstances surrounding us.

I have a photograph of myself standing on some outside stairs alongside other children who were living with Herbert and me. In that photograph, I have a bandage-turban around my head. Apparently, I had some kind of illness. They had wrapped my head and given me a cap. This photograph was sent to my mother with a note so as not to worry her, "Alfred has scraped his head but it is nothing serious. *N'inquiete pas.*" How this letter reached my mother, I do not know, but she kept it with her and then passed it on to me years later.

The French Resistance turned Évian into one of their hiding places, and the Germans were on the lookout for their operatives, which suddenly made it a dangerous place to be if they happened to run across us, so we were forced to move yet again.

Lourdes

We went west to Lourdes, one of the most important sites in the world for Catholics. What an irony that this town became a safe haven for a group of Jewish orphans. By this time, I was about nine years old, and Herb was seven. By the time we moved, winter was fast approaching, and it would have been terribly cold to be in Évian, with the wind blowing off the lake and down from the majestic snow-covered Alps. But the weather was not much better in Lourdes.

By this time, I think my father had already been executed, but of course I was completely ignorant of this. I don't think I could have lived had I known of his fate. It was a miracle that our caregivers were able to keep up our spirits with activities and tenderness. I don't remember hearing other children crying at night, but I am sure they, like me, must have done so. What could be worse for a young boy than to be separated from his parents, even under the best of circumstances?

Lourdes is a town in southwestern France in the foothills of the Pyrenees mountains. It's known for the Sanctuaire Notre-Dame de Lourdes, or the Domain, a major Catholic pilgrimage site. Each year, thousands of devout Catholics visit the Grotto of Massabielle (Grotto of Apparitions) where, in 1858, the Virgin Mary is said to have appeared seventeen times to a young girl by the name of Bernadette, who was just fourteen years old and suffering from cholera. The Virgin Mary is said to have instructed Bernadette to build a shrine there and to enclose a grotto. In the grotto, pilgrims drink or bathe in water flowing from a spring, and the waters are supposed to have curative properties for all those who come with maladies—the crippled, the sick, and the infirm. There is a fantastic basilica there as well as the grotto, and the church is served by the Sisters of Charity of Nevers, the order that Bernadette joined to become a nun. The nuns all wore a blue habit and a wimple covering their heads. Their habit has not changed even into the twenty-first century.

This order is known for serving the poor, sick, and helpless. The same order established a hospital for the pilgrims visiting Lourdes who needed medical care in combination with religious ministration. This hospital was located on the grounds of the basilica. The complex consisted of the hospital and another building for administration, a clinic, and housing for the sisters. There was also an order of priests who directed the religious services in the basilica.

The city of Lourdes and its neighbor Tarbes became an important sanctuary for Jews and others escaping the Germans. A historian describes how many good people in Lourdes, including the clergy as well as city officials, risked their lives to save Jewish children and others fleeing from the Nazis until the Liberation. Some even lost their lives, such as Monsieur Trélut. I am including this long excerpt because it touches upon so many aspects of the situation in Lourdes at the time that we were there:

> Lourdes, with its many hotels, was a perfect place to bring together children and protect them from bombing. In late 1943 children began to be moved to Lourdes and the surrounding district from the Marseille and Toulon region in anticipation of a possible Allied landing on the coast of Provence.... About 2,000 such children were evacuated to Lourdes and were well received by the inhabitants of Lourdes who were well used to welcoming people of all nations....
>
> Several of the town and village mayors, town clerks and teachers were involved in providing false identity papers for those most in need, including those residents resisting being sent to Germany by the dreaded S.T.O. (Compulsory Work Order). The local mayors and town halls also helped by providing food or organizing food collections.... Monsieur Maurice Trélut was mayor of Tarbes between 1935 and September 1944. During the

German Occupation M. Trélut was the first link in establishing a network of refugees from the hospital in Tarbes....

Many of these refugees M. Trélut was able to send to Mother Anne-Marie Llobet, Mother Superior of the Daughters of Charity. Mother Llobet took charge of placing the children in residential schools across Tarbes while their parents were given work at the hospital. Persecuted Jews from Poland, Romania or Germany who did not speak any French were given false papers categorizing them as "deaf and dumb" or "mentally deficient." This explained away the fact they could not speak or understand French. By such ways and means, many were able to escape deportation and remain free until the day of Liberation....

By such ways and means, many were able to escape deportation and remain free until the day of Liberation. Unfortunately, this was not to be so for Maurice Trélut. His "complicity" was discovered and he was arrested by the Gestapo. In July 1944 Maurice Trélut was deported to Buchenwald where he was executed in September of that year. By the time of M. Trélut's death the High Pyrenees had been liberated. His sacrifice had not been in vain. Many of those M. Trélut had been able to help during his tenure as mayor had managed to survive the war.[11]

My first memory of the town of Lourdes is living in a building that was on a narrow street near the fast-flowing Gave de Pau

[11] Ritsonvaljos, "The Liberation of Lourdes (August 1944," *The Second World War* (blog), May 8, 2011, https://2ndww.blogspot.com/2011/05/liberation-of-lourdes-august-1944.html

river. The building was originally intended as a pension for tourists. I think it was on the other side of the river from the basilica, but a ways up the river. I lived with other boys and girls on the upper floors of the pension. As I recall, everyone living in the pension, including the adults, were Jewish.

Next door to us were German air force officers. By this time, the Germans had mobilized military personnel to the south of France in anticipation of a possible invasion of Allied Forces from northern Africa (the second theater of World War II). They were no longer just occupying northern and central France.

All the children hiding in Lourdes were told not to speak to any of the German military. It was the wintertime and we used to have snowball fights with them. I remember putting rocks in my snowballs. The Germans were nice to us, though. Even the pilots who dropped bombs all over European cities during the war were very friendly to us. They might just have been letting off steam with a few orphan kids whom they did not suspect of being Jewish.

Eventually I was moved out of the pension and situated on the grounds of the basilica with the nuns and the priests. Among the many ironies of my survival was that a Jewish boy was being sheltered on the grounds of a Catholic holy site.

My brother was kept at the pension. We were separated as an act of preservation. The OSE was afraid that Herbert, being younger than me, might say something to tip off the German military and thus put both of our lives at risk. If we were separated, the theory was that at least one of us would be saved. Naturally it was a terrible hardship for me to leave my brother, especially when I had promised my parents that I would, as the older son, take care of him, no matter what. Now how was I going to do that? It caused me a lot of pain, as I felt I was shirking my responsibility to him. I don't think that the aid workers explained to me their strategy. At this time—as at so many others—I was at the mercy of those who were watching over us, without fully understanding what was happening. Secrecy was our best defense.

The Order of Nuns kept me sheltered in the hospital they ran, the Accueil Notre-Dame, on the grounds of the basilica. They knew that I was Jewish, but they thought it was their duty not only to me but to God to protect me. There were many other Catholic orders throughout France during this time who believed as they did. Perhaps they had an extra layer of protection against the Nazis because they were religious servants, although the Nazis hated the Catholics—not as much as they hated the Jews, but with considerable vehemence. In many Catholic schools throughout Europe where the Nazis held sway, teachers were forced to take down crosses and put up swastikas and photographs of Hitler in place of images of their Lord Jesus Christ.

The priest at the basilica and I took many walks together on the grounds and talked. I told him, "I am scared to be here because I am Jewish."

He was extremely kind to me and told me not to worry. I resented having to go to Sunday services in the basilica every week. He said, "I sympathize with you, but you have to go to mass for your own safety, and you have to kneel. Don't make yourself obvious. If the German soldiers come here, you will just blend in with the rest of the children. You will resemble a good Catholic boy, *n'est-ce pas?*"

I hated putting up a front. I told him that a Jew is not allowed to kneel in a church, that I didn't like it and I didn't want to do it, and I was very uncomfortable and resented it. I also knew that Jews do not believe in the Trinity—the Father, the Son, and the Holy Ghost. There is only God.

The priest listened to me with great compassion and tolerance. He responded, "At least we don't make you go to catechism." He may have said this with a sympathetic smile. I guess the message was that catechism was reserved for true Catholics. I, like many other Jewish children in other parts of France, was taught to make the sign of the cross, to say certain prayers, to genuflect, and to take Communion (which I refused to do) so that we would not be found out.

And then, of course, my name was Alfred LaCroix. What more of a Catholic name could I have been given?

The basilica had few visitors because of the war—people were afraid of being hit by a bomb, or of enemy troops roaming the countryside. Practically all the visitors to the basilica were German officers who were stationed in Lourdes and the surrounding areas. Only German soldiers and officers went into the grotto at the time.

On Sundays, called by the ringing of the bells that could be heard throughout Lourdes, they would come in their uniforms to attend the religious services at the basilica. What hypocrites, murderers, pigs. How could these people pretend to follow Christian values and charities, and how could they be seeking the help of their God and of their Church and of a priest for salvation, for peace, for forgiveness, or for whatever they were seeking in their individual prayers? They were murderers.

If they were entitled to such forgiveness, what was the Catholic Church and its clerics, bishops, cardinals, and the Pope doing for their victims? I don't remember my reaction to seeing the German military at the time, but when I look back, I recognize the hypocrisy of praying in church and then targeting Jews for deportation and murder, hand in hand with the French police who did the bidding of the Nazis. At any moment I could have been found out. Anyone could have turned around and told the authorities that the nuns were harboring a Jewish boy, but they did not. It was surely out of the goodness of their hearts.

There were children who became my friends at Lourdes. We used to "play" Catholic services. I would be the priest, and the other children would be the nuns or the congregants, and then we would switch roles. No one told us to do this, but we had no toys, so these services were like games we made up. We filled in for what we were missing. I did not think it was that strange that I should play a priest since I had seen my grandfather and my father conducting religious services when I was younger; the only difference was that they were Jewish services and not Catholic. How true our pretending was to the actual services we were mimicking, I have no idea, but we had certainly attended services enough to have some idea of the roles we played. I am surprised that the priest and the nuns did not try to convert me from Judaism to Catholicism, as was the case elsewhere during the war, particularly in Poland, but they did not. Perhaps they sensed that my religion was very important to me, or they respected the fact that I was born Jewish and that it would be wrong to do so.

During the winter months it was extremely cold in Lourdes. The wind and snow blew upon the town from the Pyrenees, a rugged mountain range between France and Spain. The nuns had no trouble finding clothes for us because generous people donated clothing whenever the nuns asked. They emphasized that they needed clothing for the orphans in their care. After all, there were many good Christians who willingly helped even when they suspected that some of these orphans might have been Jewish. That is one of the universal lessons of my experience that I have always carried with me. Lourdes was one of my way stations to freedom. If it had not been for the kindness of the nuns and the priests, I would surely have ended up a casualty of Nazi butchers and murderers.

Arrangements were made for me to spend time with an adult, like a foster parent, for one day or so on each weekend in Lourdes. I had the good luck to be picked by a Jewish single woman. She was delighted and loved the fact that she could pamper me and look after me. I asked her to take my brother with me. I cried and begged until she relented.

She did so, but reluctantly. It meant she had to spend money for a third ticket if we went to the movies and feed him during the day when we were together. On Saturday or Sunday of each week, we went to her home, and she would fix us meals and take us on outings to places that were safe for us to be.

* * *

There is a hole in the grotto wall at Lourdes where the Virgin Mary appeared and spoke to Bernadette, and that is where I stood. There was water trickling down from the rocks, and if you touched it, you were supposed to be cured of whatever illness you had. I went into the grotto and prayed. While I was there, I was so lonely. I was separated from my mother and father and my brother. When I went to bed at night, I cried myself to sleep worrying about my brother and missing my parents, wondering if they were still alive. I struggled to accept the reality of my situation and the painful separation from my parents, the people I loved most in the world.

My caretaker to whom I was assigned to spend weekends with really loved me, though. When we left Lourdes, she asked me to promise to write to her. She asked me this in the presence of another lady friend. The two of them had a conversation in which one of them said to the other, "Children do not remember their promises, or they are too lazy to write."

I never wrote to her. It probably would have been too painful for me. How attached to her I became, I do not recall. I suspect that I did not really love her. I had moved around so much that it was difficult for me to develop an attachment to any one person. I might even have deemed it disloyal to my mother and father. I certainly did not want anyone to replace them in my heart. If I had loved someone else, it might have meant that I had given up the wish that my parents were still alive and waiting for Herbert and me to be returned to them in Saint-Pardoux. I don't know how many times I imagined falling into my parents' arms, being kissed by them, and being told that we were now truly safe. It was a dream that I replayed in my head time and time again and a way for me to cope when I became depressed and despondent. Another reason I did not send her a letter is that I probably did not know how to write very well, since my schooling was constantly being interrupted. I wonder how and when I learned how to write. I was a fast learner, so whatever lessons I had, I used to their best advantage. But by the age of ten, when I should have mastered writing, I was still backward because my education was almost nonexistent. Or, if I am being hard on myself, it might have been simple laziness.

Herbert and I stayed in Lourdes longer than we did any other hiding place, and longer than at the original summer camp. I can't say that it felt like home, but we got used to it. It was a lively place because of the religious activity, and our caretakers made it feel special. We were both a little sad to leave, even though the circumstances were anything but sad.

In October 1944, Herbert and I were moved by the OSE from Lourdes to Tarbes, a neighboring city twenty-three kilometers away. The OSE deemed it was safe to do so. I shall always be grateful to the nuns and the priest in Lourdes. I don't know if I had it in my ten-year-old mind to return someday to thank these righteous people for what they did to save us. Their goodness was immeasurable, and they protected us while risking their own lives.

* * *

On June 6, 1944, the United States military forces landed on the beaches of Normandy and began their attack against German forces who were stationed on the cliffs. This was the largest seaborne invasion in military history. As the Americans along with their allies advanced, the Germans knew that the tide of the war was turning against them. News of the Allied victory on D-Day spread, raising the hopes of those French who wished only to see the Germans defeated.

On the morning of June 10, 1944, the citizens of Oradour-sur-Glane, located to the north of Lourdes, woke up to what they thought would be another normal day. Around 2:00 p.m., under the command of SS-Sturmbannführer Adolf Diekmann, somewhere between 120 and 200 soldiers of the Panzer regiment Der Führer encircled the town, blocking all entrances and exits and murdering 632 people by gunshot and fire. Many of the townspeople were trapped inside a church, and several priests died along with their congregants. This action was launched as punishment for the town's collective resistance against the Germans. Without question, the people who were protecting us learned of this unimaginable tragedy and feared that the same fate might befall them, despite the Allied victory on the Normandy beaches and the advance of the American troops inland.[12]

Less than two months later, the Allies executed Operation Dragoon, invading Provence in southern France on August 15, 1944, attacking German troops and liberating the cities and towns in that region.

And then, after more than four years of Nazi occupation, Paris was liberated by the French Second Armored Division and the United States Fourth Infantry Division in a coordinated effort, with General Charles de Gaulle as the symbolic and true hero of liberation. Throughout the war years, his voice from London assured the French: "We are going to regain our independence. We are going to expel these people." The Germans barely resisted liberation efforts in Paris. General Dietrich von Choltitz, commander of the German garrison, defied Hitler's order to blow up Paris's landmarks and burn the city to the ground before its liberation. Choltitz signed a formal surrender on the afternoon of August 26, 1944, and General Charles de Gaulle led a joyous march down the Champs Élysées through the Arc de Triomphe, symbolizing the end of the German occupation of northern and central France. He said in his radio address:

---

[12] Sarah Farmer, "Martyred Village: Commemorating the Massacre at Oradour-sur-Glane," *The National WWII Museum – New Orleans* (November 2018): https://www.nationalww2museum.org/war/articles/oradour-sur-glane-martyred-village.

Why do you wish us to hide the emotion which seizes us all, men and women, who are here, at home, in Paris that stood up to liberate itself and that succeeded in doing this with its own hands? Since the enemy which held Paris has capitulated into our hands, France returns to Paris, to her home. She returns bloody, but quite resolute. She returns there enlightened by the immense lesson, but more certain than ever of her duties and of her rights.... we will keep fighting until the final day, until the day of total and complete victory. Long live France.[13]

De Gaulle reminded his listeners that the Germans still remained on French soil and proclaimed that their forces must be defeated and France in its entirety reclaimed, along with the rest of German-occupied Europe.

By September 1944, the Germans surrendered its 339 troops to the south under the command of Commandant Kulitszcher, and the territory of Vichy France was returned to France. The puppet Vichy government was disbanded.

I have a vague memory of making little tricolored flags and waving them out the window in celebration of the liberation. With the Germans effectively vanquished by the Allies from France, the OSE deemed it safe to bring Herbert and me out of hiding. But where were we to go? Were my parents alive? And if not, who would take care of us? I was afraid to know the answers to these questions.

Tarbes

Herbert and I were placed with two separate Christian family in Tarbes, a city that was larger than Lourdes but in the same

---

[13] http://witnify.com/charles-de-gaulles-paris-liberated-speech/

general region near the Spanish-French border. (It was eventually given the Croix de Guerre in recognition of its brave stand against the Nazis.) The war was still raging in other parts of Europe, and total victory would not be declared against Germany and its Axis partners until May 1945. But in the meantime, the yoke of German dominance had been lifted from France. The country went about reestablishing its democratic institutions, rebuilding its bombed cities, and restoring its economy with the assistance of the United States and other Allied countries.

I didn't like my foster family in Tarbes. My brother got along much better with his. I suspect that I was carrying a lot of psychological baggage, and I was uncertain what our future might be. We still had no word about our parents, and there was talk of being sent to Palestine, which I knew only from our time at summer camp as a place on a map marked by twinkling blue lights.

Surely this plan was a sign that our parents must be dead. Otherwise, why would our caregivers even consider sending us so far away from France? Or maybe my parents were in Palestine. I had no answers, and I was very confused. Herbert, who was eight years old, took it in stride. I did know that many Jews were leaving for Palestine, feeling a strong personal connection to the country. It was deemed the Holy Land, the birthplace of Judaism (as well as the birthplace of Christianity and Islam). What better place to plant our feet, argued some. I thought it was a terrible idea. It didn't interest me at all. I am sure that every time Palestine was mentioned I became more adamant that I would not go there. I think my foster family became annoyed with me, even if they were being paid to give us a roof over our heads. I was seen as a very uncooperative child, which may not have been far from the truth.

One day a woman from the OSE visited me in my foster home in Tarbes. She had visited me from time to time to make sure that I was being well cared for. She did the same for my brother and other Jewish children who were sheltered in Tarbes and the surrounding towns.

She said, "I have some news for you about your mother."

She stared right into my face. I thought she was going to confirm that my mother was dead. She said it in such a way that I have relived that moment so many times. I braced myself for the worst news I could have received. I am sure that my eyes were already filling with tears. I held my breath, waiting for the words that I had prepared myself for.

My mother sitting in front of her sewing machine in Saint-Pardoux-de-Breuil, France.
On her table is a photograph of my brother and me taken in Chabannes.
She kept this photo with her to remind herself that we were alive.

My brother Herbert and me taken in Chabannes where we were cared
for by the Oeuvre de Secours aux Enfants (OSE).

With a group of other children at summer camp, July 1943, hidden from the police and Nazis. I am seated cross-legged in the front row, at age 8.

Taking hiking trips into the mountains with other hidden children.

Group photo on stairs of our temporary lodging in Evian. I have a bandage on my head from an accident. My brother Herbert is second boy from the left in the front row.

CHAPTER 9

"Your Mother Is Alive"

The woman from the aid agency said, "We found your mother."

I was speechless for what seemed like hours but was only a few seconds of total astonishment.

What joy, what elation, what a miracle that my mother had been found! I cannot describe the great pain and joy I simultaneously felt in that moment. It had been what I had been praying for, hoping for, and imagining too many times to count.

I don't know why it had taken the aid agency so long to locate my mother, especially since she had never left the Saint-Pardoux area. It's possible that they kept us separated for both of our safety, and they kept my mother's whereabouts a secret from us— and ours from her—so that we would not try to contact each other and thereby put ourselves in danger. The Germans could have intercepted our communication and tracked both of us down. I do know that the OSE gave my mother pictures of my brother and me to assure her that we were safe and well cared for. She kept those pictures with her throughout our separation and for the rest of her life. I now have them in safe keeping. One that was especially precious to her was the picture of Herbert and me in our sabots and berets—two *mignon garçons français.*

I didn't ask if my father was alive. I was too overcome. I expected that I would hear about him from my mother once we were all reunited, wherever and whenever that would occur. All I wanted to know was when we would see our mother again.

After gathering our few possessions and saying goodbye and *merci* to our foster families and to the OSE volunteers, Herbert and I were given tickets and put on a train from Tarbes back to Marmande. The Germans had been evacuated from France and it was now safe for us to travel. Whether all the Germans had been rooted out was not assured. Some might have gone into hiding with the aid of those French who were still sympathetic to the Nazis.

I remember being on the train. I could hear the wheels turning on the tracks and with each turn I was coming closer and closer to seeing my mother again. I was unbearably impatient. The train finally arrived in Marmande. We got off the train and once again stood on the platform where I had last seen my mother and father, waving goodbye to them as we set off for what we thought would be a few weeks of summer camp. On that same platform stood my mother. I ran to her and hugged and kissed her, as did my brother. Our faces were wet with tears of joy and gratitude. We had been separated for two and a half years, which to a ten-year-old feels like a lifetime. I am sure I had grown an inch or two, as had my brother, but I don't remember my mother commenting on this.

My mother's friend, Madame Radzinsky, who owned a clothing store in Marmande, accompanied my mother. She asked if I recognized my mother. I said that I thought she was fatter than when I had last seen her. My mother laughed. She did not think my comment rude. To me, it was a sign that she was healthy, since food had been scarce in Lourdes and we often had trouble getting enough to eat.

Our reunion was marvelous. It was what I had been praying for, hoping for, wishing for. The thought that I might not see my mother again had often brought me almost to the point of desperation. And what about my father?

At the moment of our reunion, I suspect that I realized that I didn't have a father anymore. I asked my mother how he was and where he was, hoping that he was alive and waiting at home or perhaps also on a train on his way back to join us. She answered that she did not know, but her silence and the tortured look in her eyes told me everything I needed to know. I can only imagine how difficult it was for her to stay silent about my father's fate. In fact, she might have known very little about what happened to him at that time. It was only through the research I conducted many years later that I learned all the facts of his final months.

How did my mother survive when the French authorities regularly searched for and seized immigrant Jews during those two and a half years? The Ros family, our loyal Italian-born neighbors, hid and protected my mother in Saint-Pardoux. They fed and sheltered her and provided her companionship. In exchange, she sewed and repaired their clothing, which she did for other neighbors whenever possible.

When the French gendarmes came around, the Ros family hid her in a secret wall in the owner's little château on the land that they farmed. None of them ever allowed anyone to harm her. Because they did such a good job hiding my mother, though, the Jewish aid agency was unable to locate her.

Throughout our own exile, I knew little about the war. I knew that it was happening. I knew that the Germans were trying to dominate Europe. But I was too young to understand the details, and our caretakers tried to shield us from the news. As it turned out, the Nazis were not quite defeated by the time our family was reunited. But they were on the retreat. After heavy fighting on the eastern front in early 1945, Soviet forces neared Adolf Hitler's command bunker in central Berlin. On April 30, 1945, Hitler committed suicide. Within days, Berlin fell to the Soviets. German armed forces surrendered unconditionally in the West on May 7 and in the East on May 9, 1945.

The joy throughout Europe and even in our distant corner of southwest France was overwhelming. But I had an added reason to be joyous—or, at least, hopeful.

On that day, I still imagined that maybe my father would be liberated and return to Saint-Pardoux. We waited, or at least I did.

Some people did come back. We heard stories of the liberation of the concentration camps by American and Russian troops and of tearful reunions among Jews and other victims of the Nazis across Europe. I thought of all the children whose parents were returned to them or who were returned to their parents and imagined their elation—just like the elation I had felt when we returned to our mother. Then those stories quieted down, and then they stopped altogether. We heard no word about my father's fate, but I am sure my mother kept asking; she might have learned the truth from another inmate at Majdanek who survived. She might have been told, "Yes, I saw your beloved husband, Simche, pushed into the ditch, but I could do nothing to help him." What an image to have to carry with you for the rest of your life.

I can only guess how people who did survive the camps lived with these images and the feelings of guilt that they had somehow survived when most others died in such horrific ways.

The liberation of France in its entirety was a mental liberation for us. We did not need to live in fear anymore. We did not need to wonder where we were or where we were going. We did not need to mind our manners among strangers, however kind they were, who looked after us. We did not have to hide our identities or use made-up names. We returned to our modest lives in Saint-Pardoux among friends such as the Ros and Berney families and Gérard Guillot.

We were once again Albert and Herbert Lakritz, not LaCroix. It would take me many more years to discover why the name that I was born with—Weber—had been taken away from me and from my family.

When we spoke of the war and the Vichy government, we took to referring to the German soldiers as "*Boche.*" The word came from a French slang word *alboche*, which was a combination of *allemand*, meaning a German person, and *caboche*, meaning either "head" or "cabbage." It evolved into an offensive epithet that the Nazi soldiers fully deserved. We uttered it with reckless abandon and exuberance. There were no SS officers to police our language or thoughts.

Herb's and my survival is a testament to the goodness of other people. They protected us from all possible major ills. They are the righteous. Others acted out of other motives and needs. They can be viewed by the times, circumstances, and their choices. In total, 72,400 Jewish children in France survived the war: 62,000 stayed with or were entrusted by their parents to others, and 8,000 to 10,000 were saved by organizations like the one that saved us.

Everyone had a choice to make—some people made the choice to help us, while others turned a blind eye and still others colluded with the enemy—that is the nature of free will and of human frailty.

* * *

Even though the war was officially over in Europe and we were free to go anywhere we pleased, we didn't really have anywhere to go. We didn't know what happened to our relatives living in Europe, and the Fass family was thousands of miles away. My mother did not have a profession or trade that required her to be any one place in particular. Most of all, we did not necessarily feel our freedom. Yes, we had moved around a great deal from the time I was essentially a refugee to the time I had my tenth birthday in France. But we had never moved by choice. We moved because we had to. The idea of moving by choice was unimaginable. And, of course, we had essentially no money. We couldn't afford train tickets to Paris, Lyon, or any other city that might have appealed to us.

We really had no option but to stay in France—in Marmande. The one benefit we had was due to a gesture of atonement—that may be the best way to put it—on the part of the French government. Because of my father's contributions to the Resistance, he was declared a victim of the war "who fought for the French." Herb and I were designated "orphans of the country." Even though our mother was alive, the government recognized the hardships a family faces when the breadwinner is gone. Monsieur Gérard Guillot, the administrator of Marmande, arranged for our mother to receive a pension as the widow of a hero of the Resistance. The German government also offered reparations to Jewish families some years later, but I refused to accept any money from the German government.

We did, though, still have family in California. After our reunification, our mother again made an immediate application to immigrate to the United States. We were stateless. We were poor. We had nothing but one another. The Fass family once again served as our sponsors. Hopefully this time we would have the necessary documentation and the funds to leave. But, *comme toujours*, there were complications.

My mother had been born in an area that was ceded to Poland at the end of World War I. Because of her birthplace, we were considered part of the Polish immigration quota to the United States. Poland had fallen behind the Iron Curtain as part of the settlement crafted after the war, giving Poles a low and limited priority among refugees, even if we had suffered through the Holocaust. The United States treated Poles—which we weren't, of course—as less desirable than Germans. The fact that Herbert and I were born in Kiel, Germany, didn't give us any priority by the United States immigration service. Our application was dictated by our mother's birthplace, which was questionable since the borders kept changing before, during, and after World War I.

I didn't know the word "irony" at the time, but to this day, "ironic" is how I think of that situation, since so many Polish Jews were targeted by the Germans and suffered the worst losses of Jewish lives of any country during the war. But the United States had established its priorities, and the immigration quotas were based on diplomatic and political games. There were also enemies of the United States who escaped Europe after the war— hiding out in Latin American countries, protected by local police until they were ferreted out by Nazi hunters who were determined to bring them to trial.

Between 1945 and 1949, war crimes tribunals were held in Nuremberg, Germany, to convict the most egregious perpetrators who had been caught by Nazi hunters such as Serge Klarsfeld and Simon Wiesenthal. The common defense of these Nazi butchers is that they were "just following orders," as if they had no choice but to do Hitler's bidding, when the truth was anything but that.

Lower-level criminals have been tried even into the twenty-first century, including concentration camp guards who were living "quiet lives" in the United States.[14] In 1961, at a court in Jerusalem, Adolf Eichmann, one of Hitler's preeminent henchmen, was tried and convicted of war crimes. Prosecuting attorneys brought Holocaust survivors as witnesses against Eichmann, giving irrefutable testimony of Eichmann's debauchery. The eyes of the world were riveted on the proceedings, which were telecast. In a final attempt at clemency, Eichmann repeated the defense of others, "I was just following orders." There may still be a few elderly Nazis who continue to live in the United States and Latin America undercover until death claims them.

* * *

While my mother searched for ways that we could legally immigrate to the United States, we settled into a semblance of normal life in the French countryside. We moved into the very same building we had lived in before the war on the Boulevard de Mare, across from a warehouse and near the very location where

---

[14] In mid-1945, France, the Soviet Union, the United Kingdom, and the United States agreed to convene a joint tribunal in Nuremberg, with the Nuremberg Charter as its legal instrument. Between November 20, 1945 and October 1, 1946, the International Military Tribunal (IMT) tried twenty-one of the most important surviving leaders of Nazi Germany in the political, military, and economic spheres, as well as six German organizations. The purpose of the trial was not just to convict the defendants but also to assemble irrefutable evidence of Nazi crimes, offer a history lesson to the defeated Germans, and delegitimize the traditional German elite.

my father had set up the viewing stands for the Vichy officials for the *fête* years before. The apartment, which was owned by the city, was allocated to my mother by Gérard Guillot. His son became my brother's good friend. They used to play soccer together. I had no interest in soccer and did not join them.

Our apartment faced the boulevard. It had a large room in front and another room across the staircase. The building itself dated back to the fifteenth century and has since been declared a historic site. I can imagine tourists looking up at our window without any knowledge of who lived there—two young boys and their widowed mother who was desperately trying to leave France for the United States.

The only other viable option was Palestine. Jewish aid organizations helped arrange and pay for the relocation of Jews to their ancestral homeland—in anticipation of the creation of the State of Israel. Moving to Palestine was a dream come true for many Jews. But my mother had no interest in immigrating there. She wanted to be with her father's brother, my great-uncle Max Fass, and his children and grandchildren.

I have a letter from HIAS headquarters in New York that was written to my great-uncle in Oakland, California, dated September 25, 1945, asking for certain documents to begin the process of bringing my mother, my brother, and me to the United States. The letter mentions receipt of $425 for each person's passage on a boat to the United States. That money must have been furnished by the Fass family, because my mother certainly did not have that much money.

I wonder what my mother thought of living in the same building we had lived in with our father—to live where my father had conducted religious services for the other refugee Jews. Surely, they evoked sincere prayers for salvation and guidance from the Almighty. Surely at that moment, they were all observant Jews. And, just as surely, most of them perished. Their prayers did them no good in this world.

Where was God? Did He answer their prayers for salvation? Each of us must answer this question for ourselves. It is a struggle to answer in the affirmative when so many died, when so many were tortured, when so many had their livelihoods taken away from them. And yet, perhaps there would have been fewer survivors like my mother, Herbert, and me, if God had not somehow intervened. But I cannot say with any real certainty. All I know is that we were spared because of the kindness of others. It was surely a miracle!

My mother—at the age of thirty-nine—had the sole responsibility for ensuring the survival of her ten- and eight-year-old sons. Would her prayers be answered when the men who had also prayed were ignored and slaughtered? What did my mother think? What did she fear? She toiled like only a determined mother can in order to nourish, educate, and stimulate curiosity in her sons. We were her hope for the future. Had we not survived, there is no telling what my mother might have done in her hour of desperation.

These questions persist in my mind because I never discussed them with my mother. The war had been a force beyond our control and nearly beyond our comprehension. No amount of discussion could have changed it or its aftermath. No amount of discussion could have brought back my father or restored our home in Kiel.

Years later, I complained to a historian and journalist, telling him, "We were lambs sacrificed to the Vichy policy of collaboration." I did not experience what is referred to as survivor's guilt, but rather an anger so intense that at times it became overwhelming. I hated my birthplace, I hated the Nazis, I hated their accomplices. I carried deep sorrow for my mother and father and great pain in my heart. My mother focused on the present—on our immediate needs. Neither Herb nor I had the wherewithal to talk about the war with anyone, even our mother. We just wanted to focus on the future. What was past was past.

But, of course, that was not true. I have carried the scars of my past throughout my life, and I have the deepest of feelings to this day when I think about and talk about some of the events. When I write about what happened to me in this memoir, I sometimes have to hold back tears, and once in a while I just let them flow because they overtake me. I wonder if anyone reading my words will feel sympathy or empathy for what I went through.

CHAPTER 10

A Tailor's Apprentice

My mother enrolled Herb and me in a nonsectarian school in Marmande. She was very concerned that we catch up with our grade level after having missed so many years of education while we were moving from place to place without any formal schooling. She was mindful of our future and wanted to make sure that we would be prepared to support ourselves as successful adults someday. She had traversed the river of survival and was now floating toward a better future. It is amazing to me that she imagined a normal life for us, which included getting the education that we had been denied.

The school Herb and I attended was *un école laïque*. These are schools without religious identification or teaching—what are known as secular schools. That approach came from the age of Napoleon I, when he initiated a culture of tolerance in France. No matter what his wrongs or excesses may have been, he was responsible for some good policies—certainly for Jewish citizens. This is a throwback to the French Revolution, when the French people rejected nobility, classes, dictatorship, and government by decrees without the consent of the people, as had existed under the monarchy.

Napoleon gave the Jews all the rights accruing to French citizens. But he also insisted that Jews give up their money-lending activities. This was an example of what some considered Napoleon's ulterior motives. Orthodox Rabbi Berel Wein claimed that Napoleon was interested primarily in seeing the Jews assimilate into mainstream French life, rather than prosper as a distinct community: "Napoleon's outward tolerance and fairness toward Jews was actually based upon his grand plan to have them disappear entirely by means of total assimilation, intermarriage, and conversion."[15]

I reluctantly attended school in Marmande for about two years, during which time I got into a lot of trouble and was very bored. The teachers shamed me and hit me with a ruler for misbehaving and for my obstinance and indifference.

My brother and I attended class with other students, but we didn't have what the other children had. For example, we didn't have marbles.

During recess, the boys would play a marble game where you stack marbles on top of each other in a sort of pyramid and then, standing a few feet away, your competitor would throw a marble with his thumb and his hand aiming at your stack. If he missed, the boy who had stacked his marbles against the wall would keep it and gain a marble. If he knocked it down, then you collected those marbles. My brother and I didn't have store-bought marbles, so we made our own out of baked clay. We painted them different colors, hoping that we would be able to throw them and

[15] "Napoleon and the Jews," *Wikipedia*, last modified February 5, 2023, https://en.wikipedia.org/wiki/Napoleon_and_the_Jews.

knock down the stack of marbles and acquire marbles in that manner. I don't know how this worked, but I remember playing this game frequently. I may have been able to pocket a few, because I certainly did not have the money to buy a set. Playing marbles was one of the few activities I enjoyed at *l'école laïque*—I had no interest in the academic subjects.

When I was thirteen and no longer obligated by French law to attend school, I told my mother I wanted to drop out. She said that if I didn't go to school, I would have to learn a trade and make myself useful. She didn't like the idea of my being idle and getting into trouble. To her credit, she did not force me to stay in school or compare me to my younger brother, who was eager to learn. He very easily adapted to the rigors and rules of school, whereas I rebelled. I think his age made him more malleable, while I, as a budding teenager, entered an obstinate period where I only wanted to hold my own counsel and did not want to listen to the teachers, who punished me for the smallest infraction.

What was there to do for an uncooperative thirteen-year-old boy like me?

Many Jews in Marmande were involved in the clothing business. The Radzinskys—who were originally from Alsace-Lorraine—ran a store called Chemin de Fer ("iron horse," i.e. "locomotive"), which sold clothing to farmers and laborers. Another family, the Alcos, had a clothing store next door. They were both around the corner from city hall and the police station.

My mother had become an expert seamstress during the war as a way to support herself. She did good work, and people liked her. She was a quiet, nice person. By that point, her masterpieces were a bridal dress and a groom's suit for members of the Ros family. Once she had made this special clothing, others in Saint-

Pardoux asked that she do the same for them. She also made other items of clothing for working in the fields and attending church, when people wear their Sunday best.

Given her connections with people in the clothing business and her friendship with Madame Radzinsky, she suggested that I become an apprentice tailor. Down the street from where we lived was a tailor named Monsieur Paul Robert who owned a shop. He was a very stylish man and wore his clothes beautifully. He walked around town advertising his clothing.

I became an apprentice alongside his son, Daniel. He was a decent tailor, but he was a magnificent roller-skater. He should have been in the Olympics. He would roller-skate up and down the boulevard, gliding along and doing tricks. That wasn't easy back then. The roller skates had metal wheels, so they did not skim smoothly along the pavement and cobblestones. It was easy to trip, but Daniel rarely took a tumble—he was that good.

Another boy from Marmande named Jean-Pierre Delpech didn't want to continue with school either and became an apprentice for Monsieur Robert as well. We had an interesting group. There was a tailor from Hungary or somewhere in the Baltic area who worked in Monsieur Robert's shop. He was the most skilled tailor other than Monsieur Robert himself.

And there was Madame Éclair, who was a widow, and a Madame Courder, who was a seamstress. None of these people were Jewish, but in that shop there was no prejudice, and the tailoring was outstanding. Only top-quality men's suits were turned out of Monsieur Robert's shop. I was generally given the job of sewing the lapels on men's suits and topstitching. I was not a good apprentice, but he encouraged me. One of the rules Monsieur Robert imparted to me, which I have carried for the rest of my life, is that if you do something, do it to the best of your ability. Don't cut corners. He never accepted mediocrity from anyone who worked for him.

I really wasn't interested in learning to become a tailor for the same reason that I wasn't interested in continuing my schooling— it was boring to me. I was, however, interested in learning English. I knew that my mother had applied for asylum, and I held out hope that we could be accepted and whisked away to the United States at any moment. I wanted to be ready. Unfortunately, I had no one with whom to practice English. I wrote to the American embassy in Paris to ask for books and instructional materials. They sent some books, which made me excited. I did not learn much since I had no one to practice with, and my mother did not have the money to hire a tutor. But I had a facility for languages, so when the time came, I picked up English quickly, just as I had picked up the patois of Saint-Pardoux and learned French.

My brother felt strongly attached to France, whereas I treated it as a waystation. Herbert was happy in France. Therefore, he had no interest in learning English, so I couldn't rely on him to help me learn and practice the language.

I did mostly menial work at Monsieur Robert's tailor shop. I kept myself occupied and chatted with one of the assistants.

Daniel Robert was an avid bicyclist, and he belonged to a bicycle federation. I joined as well, and the bicycle that I had was a heavy old hand-me-down. (My brother somehow got a better bicycle, but it was a girl's bicycle, and he was embarrassed to ride it and was somewhat jealous of mine.) I don't know how we bought this bicycle. Anyway, it was mine, and I would go on outings with a big group that included Monsieur Robert's employees. One time we went to Bordeaux and came back the same day. That was quite an outing; Bordeaux is ninety-one kilometers from Marmande.

Another time, we went on an outing for the day, and the group stopped for lunch at a restaurant. I didn't have money for lunch. I was sitting outside, eating whatever it was that my mother had made for me. Everyone else was inside the restaurant at the table eating and drinking. I looked in the window at the congenial group, but I wasn't invited to join them.

In that moment, I realized I was a stranger in their midst—an outsider, even if I worked shoulder to shoulder with them in the tailor shop. I felt anguish, but I never felt envy. I didn't envy their food, and I didn't resent them for excluding me. I was anguished over not having the money to pay for my own lunch and felt that I was inherently lower in their eyes because I was poor.

I reminded myself, though, that I was a survivor. My family's poverty was not due to laziness or immorality, on my part or my parents'. It was because we had faced the greatest evil the world has ever known. I cannot say that we defeated the evil. People far braver than me, Herbert, and my mother accomplished that. But the evil did not defeat us. So why should I be affected by being excluded from this gathering? On the scale of everything that I had endured, it was really nothing. But as a teenager I still felt excluded, and this feeling was painful. Later in life, I became a joiner. I was very social and learned the joy of being part of a group that accepted me. I never wanted to feel like an outsider again, looking through a window and seeing others enjoying a sense of camaraderie and friendship, while I sat on a stoop outside, alone.

* * *

Before long, the war became a distant memory, especially in Marmande.

Nazi regalia had never been common in Marmande. What little there was had quickly been removed. The war's impact was evident in absence—absence of people, of Jews who were taken away and young Frenchmen who fought and died—rather than in any mementos or obvious reminders. The evil that had nearly consumed Europe was quickly erased from the public's eye. Any remaining Nazi sympathizers kept their thoughts to themselves, but I'm sure they were around. It is not easy to extinguish long-held racism and bias, especially when these thoughts are taught by the Church and tied to religious beliefs.

And then there were those people who blamed the Jews for what happened in France between the wars; they thought of the Jews as thieves, taking jobs and money from the general population. They were also jealous of what the Jews had accomplished—a small minority who achieved a lot. As an example, the Rothschild family—Jews with relatives in France, England, and the former Austro-Hungarian Empire—created a mercantile network that was as rich as royalty. They owned banks, land, art treasures, and jewels befitting a monarchy that engendered jealousy among some French. And that jealousy transformed itself into unbridled hatred. It did not take very much to ignite that hatred into collaboration with the Nazis.

One reminder of the war was the presence of a certain group of broken women in Marmande. During the war, some women had offered themselves as prostitutes to Nazi soldiers. I don't think I fully understood their offense at the time. But I knew they had given comfort of some sort to the German soldiers who tormented us. They sold themselves for stockings, cigarettes, and food, if not for actual cash. These women were, I presume, desperate. Even so, I could not forgive them for what they had done. On one occasion after the war, the town of Marmande paraded several of these women—their heads shaven—through the town square to shame them. They were accused of *collaboration féminine*, or "horizontal collaboration." This practice of head shaving by *tondeurs* and marching these women through the streets went on in many French cities and towns after the liberation in 1944.[16] I was no fan of these women, and neither were my friends. Even so, the shaming seemed hypocritical to me. It was, to be honest, the kind of thing that Nazis would do.

I myself judged them, knowing what they did was wrong, but many of the people who were shaming them had colluded with the Nazis during the war, so who were they to judge them? It was hypocritical. Were they in some way trying to purge themselves of their own guilt by shaving the heads of these women? This display of cruelty made a lasting impression on me. Who was right and who was wrong? Who was good and who was evil? And how did my judgment of them affect my self-regard?

* * *

The attitude of the general public toward the Jews who had survived the war, returning from the concentration camps or from other countries such as Switzerland, and those who managed to stay had a complex attitude toward the colluders and those who turned a blind eye. Historians and politicians have grappled with this legacy. For example, de Gaulle as the returning hero to France emphasized the eternal unity of the French people and chose not to speak out at length about the phenomenon of

[16] https://en.wikipedia.org/wiki/Horizontal_collaboration

anti-Semitism. The past was the past. Here is a brilliant analysis by graduate student, Kathleen O'Rourke, regarding France's post-war years:

"The place of Jews in France is something that has been redefined throughout their history. France's national identity makes it difficult for outsiders to be accepted, but once a foreigner obtains French citizenship, then nothing else matters. **The only way the French Jews were able to remain in France and live with what happened was because they put their French identity first, in turn proving how French they truly were**" [emphasis mine].[17]

* * *

The end of the war enabled us to rediscover our faith. Of course, Herbert and I had practiced many Jewish traditions during our exile—that was the whole point of the summer camp. But practicing as a family was something different, especially in our father's absence.

Our relationship with Judaism was complicated and subtle. Judaism was one of the predominant facts of our lives. I knew of my father's and grandfather's devotion to the practice of Judaism and to the Jewish communities in which they lived. I knew that Judaism had been the reason for my family's migrations, from Galicia to Germany to France and beyond. Judaism was the reason my father was killed and the reason my brother, my mother, and I easily could have been killed as well.

And yet, we did not actively observe Judaism after my brother and I returned to Marmande and lived with our mother again, even if she had been as religious as my father when they married.

---

[17] https://scholarcommons.scu.edu/cgi/viewcontent.cgi?article=1067&context=historical-perspectives

We said occasional prayers and observed major holidays. But our practice of Judaism certainly did not live up to Orthodox standards. We did not have a thriving synagogue—not since my father left—and there were hardly any other Jews in Marmande. And, as proud as we were to be Jewish, Judaism was also associated with trauma. Throughout the war, I questioned God's benevolence, and I had many moments when I questioned whether being a devout Jew was worth the price that we had to pay. But in the end, I never denounced my religion, finding joy in renewing my practice openly and honestly. No more genuflection, no more making the sign of the cross, no more hiding behind the name LaCroix.

My mother saw to it that we had our bar mitzvahs. Above all else, she knew that it's what my father would have wanted. An older Jewish scholar named Dr. Landau who lived in the nearby city of Agen came to Marmande one day a week to teach us the benedictions and the haftorah for the bar mitzvah service. He was among the gentlest human beings I have ever known, and he treated me very kindly. My closest friend, Claude Radzinsky, who was about six months older than me, and his brother were also taking lessons from him. When Claude had his bar mitzvah, we went to Agen and had a big banquet at a restaurant. It might have been the first formal meal I'd ever had.

When it was my turn in 1947, Dr. Landau performed the service. My mother paid whatever his fees were. Of course, I'm sure that he didn't get much for coming to Marmande every week to teach a boy his bar mitzvah. Dr. Landau did it more out of religious conviction and goodness than for money. He probably thought about all the Jewish boys who perished in the concentration camps and would never get to celebrate their own bar mitzvahs.

We went to Agen for my bar mitzvah. It was a beautiful town with elegant Renaissance buildings and a Musée des Beaux-Arts. Monsieur and Madame Radzinsky and Claude attended the service, along with my mother and Herb, and then we went to a restaurant. By the time my brother had his bar mitzvah, nobody else came.

I was generally a pretty independent kid. I have always been, to a degree, stubborn and self-reliant. I am in some ways contrary and in other ways totally accepting of whatever rules and requirements are in effect. I was perfectly willing to go through bar mitzvah training. In fact, I think I was proud of this accomplishment and saw it as a connection to my father; my mother surely hoped I would see it that way. It was my formal passage into adulthood according to Jewish tradition.

My brother did not share my burdens. He had fun in the lycée and did well in his studies. He received at least one academic award. He played soccer. I did not. Instead, my friend Jean-Pierre Delpech, the other apprentice in Monsieur Robert's tailor shop, was on the rugby team for that age youth group. They were a pretty good team. He got the coach to allow me to attend practice sessions, and I went on some of the trips to play teams in other towns. Frankly, I wasn't good enough to play on the team. The coach was nice to me, though, and he allowed me to go onto the field for a play once in a while. Mainly I was a so-called "water boy." It was a special experience to be with these boys and to be on a team, to belong somewhere.

We also visited the city of Saint-Tropez, which is a fishing port on the Mediterranean. This trip for Jewish boys and girls was paid for by an aid agency. Today, Saint-Tropez is, of course, one of the most famous seaside resorts in France. Back then, it was not yet famous. But even at that time it was beginning to become a French movie colony where celebrities resided, making Saint-Tropez a chic place to visit.

I was enchanted to be there and to have a real vacation. I went down to the shore where the fishermen docked their boats. A staircase led down to the water. I reached the bottom and was about to dive into the water when I looked up at the top of the stairs and saw a man whom I recognized right away. He was one of the greatest French actors of his day. I recognized him because I spent a good amount of time at the movies in Marmande. We had very little money, and what little I had, I often spent there. And when I didn't have money for movies, I would go and stand at the front door of the movie house and look through the crack of the door; I would stand there stubbornly, even though I knew it was terrible to do so when other people came in to buy tickets and enter the theater. But the usher sometimes would feel sorry for me. He'd say, "Okay, you paid your dues," and he would call me and speed me into the movie.

During those years, up until age thirteen or fourteen, I enrolled in the Boy Scout movement in France. We weren't part of the regular Boy Scouts of France, which was a Catholic group; we were part of the Eclaireurs de France, which is nondenominational, without religious affiliation. ("*Eclaireurs*" is French for "scouts.") Our first meeting place was a deserted prison in the city of Marmande. It didn't have bars on the doors, but it still looked like a prison. It didn't feel like one, though, because scouting was fun and upbeat. Scouting feels a bit like the military, with ranks and drills and so forth. But it was not militaristic at all. It helped me deepen my relationship with nature and the outdoors.

Herb and I had a great time with the Scouts. We had skills to learn and badges to achieve. We went camping. We stayed outdoors in tents or barns, or in caves. We took trips by bicycle and by foot. We explored caves, where we found ancient tools and instruments that the cavemen or women of Paleolithic times used. That region of France has many caves, and it is where, shortly after the end of the war, two boys discovered the entrance to the famous Lascaux caves. It turned out that as far back as 17,000 years ago during the Upper Paleolithic period, cavemen of that region expressed themselves in fantastic animal drawings and left behind relics that were discovered beneath leaves and topsoil. (After many years of tourists tromping through the caves, the site was closed down and a replica was built representing the amazing drawings of animals and hunters.)

During the post-war years, Herb, my mother, and I spent time at the farm with the Ros family in Saint-Pardoux. The Ros family was very self-sufficient. They raised their own vegetables and had their own poultry—chicken and ducks—and cows. Some were for milk production, with others for plowing and doing other chores. They had two young children: the boy, Lino, was my age, and the girl was Herb's age. We had all sorts of fun—we even staged performances for our families.

One of the jobs we were given was to take the cows grazing. We also tended the tobacco plants. As prescribed by the French government, we picked the bottom leaves of tobacco plants to improve the quality of the tobacco. Tearing off the bottom leaves forces the upper leaves to grow more robustly. The process is called "suckering." The French government had a monopoly in tobacco, meaning we couldn't grow our own seeds, so we had to cut the tip when there was a flower, bending and removing, then collecting the dead ones. I am not sure exactly what we did with them, whether they hung the leaves and roasted them to turn them into pipe and cigarette tobacco. Inspectors would come by to make sure that we were adhering to the law. Whatever leaves were not turned over for tobacco were used as fertilizer—nothing was to go to waste.

The Ros family had grapevines for wine. The vendage was a great, fun time. We plucked the grapes off the vine and put them in the basket. Then we brought the basket to the truck, where we dumped the grapes. Of course, we'd eat whatever we wanted while we worked. Then when the grapes were brought into large wooden barrels, we were given the job of crushing them with our feet!

After a few days, while the grapes fermented in the barrels, we were allowed to taste the fruit. That juice was of course warm and very sweet—and very strong! People would come to help one another during the vendage; it was a community activity—neighbor helping neighbor from one farm to the next. They did the same for harvesting wheat and other crops during the fall.

We laid traps for rabbits, but I don't recall ever catching one. We learned to tell the difference between edible and poisonous mushrooms. We collected fantastically beautiful wild mushrooms that grow in the forests of this part of France. These mushrooms are large, dark on top, and beige or white underneath. They are a real delicacy. I remember harvesting them, and to this day I love those mushrooms. We also collected chanterelle mushrooms, which aren't as spectacular to look at but are very tasty.

My mother, Herb, and I visited the Ros family at Christmas and Easter, which were very festive times. Some members of the family would go down to the church, while others stayed at the farm. We would make butter in one of those great big wooden churns. My arms always got tired pushing the plunger up and down to turn the cream into butter. It was delicious.

I learned to work hard on the farm, learning to love vegetables and fruits; after all, they had all kinds of fruit. Apples, pears, cherries, and plums were abundant. The plums grown in this part of France are famous. The farmers put them in smokers and turned them into prunes, which were delicious.

This was when I learned to appreciate wine. Pierre Ros was a hardworking farmer. He would have soup for breakfast in the mornings, and he would pour this red wine in the soup. I asked him one day why he did that. He said that it was to cut the fat. The fat by itself was not good for you. On the other hand, we ate fat from goose, chicken liver, and we mixed chicken fat into the goose liver. My mother loved to make it for me. She would serve it with onions and some salt, and it was just delicious. We also ate bone marrow, which to my palette was another delicacy.

I can't say I was a farm boy, but I learned many aspects of farm life visiting the Ros family. I learned to appreciate what hard labor was necessary to bring food to the table and what the bounty of the earth truly meant. I will be forever grateful for these experiences.

The Ros family treated us as if we were their own flesh and blood—as if we were the nearest of kin. They must have felt that way because they had protected my mother during the war, and now they looked after Herbert and me as well.

Their eldest son, Auguste, returned from Germany. He had been arrested by the French police and turned over to the Germans, who put him in a labor camp. He was part of the Service du travail obligatoire (STO), or the compulsory work service. The Vichy government promised the French that the young men sent to Germany would acquire new skills. In the end nearly six hundred thousand young Frenchmen were drafted. Those who refused to go had to go into hiding, and those who hid them were slapped with a fine or worse.[18] He told us stories of his experiences during the war and the pranks he would play on the wife of the manager of the place where they worked. She was a flirting kind of woman, and they of course tried to flirt with her. They had different tricks. For example, they would put a mirror on the top of their shoes and put it under her skirt and tease her. I am not sure I fully understood the reason why they did this but maybe someone enlightened me at the time. After all, I was a teenager. I'm sure that the grown-ups had a good laugh hearing his stories, although perhaps they embarrassed my mother (and it is, of course, abhorrent to me in retrospect). She might not have wanted us to understand what he and his *copains* were up to.

The second son, Italo Ros, remained on the farm. He became his father's right-hand man. He educated us about sex—that men lie on women and that they don't just lie there and pass the time, that there was something going on. Now, of course, we had that education by seeing the bulls mount the cows, the roosters mounting the chickens, the male ducks mounting the female ducks, and we saw animals being born. I saw the birth, at least on one occasion, of a calf. That was really a learning experience,

---

[18] Anne Berest, *The Postcard* (Europa editions, 2023) translated by Tina Kover, p. 396.

to see it coming out of its mother. I don't know that they allowed me to stay for the whole thing, but I saw enough of it that I got the idea.

Claude Radzinsky, whose mother was my mother's closest friend, became my pal. We would spend time together on weekends. He and I discovered girls together. (Maybe I shared with him what I learned on the farm from watching the animals and listening to Italo Ros's lessons.) Claude and I sometimes went to a café in Marmande. We'd sit there, order an aperitif, and chat with the girls. We acted like big shots even if we really were little pishers. These café experiences were my civilian passage into adulthood. We talked about sex, but we didn't do it. Claude and I also went to the movies, where we probably watched scenes about sex and romance. It was a happy time for me. I had a real friend!

* * *

And then I gained another friend. An elderly man by the name of Georges Blancher lived across the hall from us in our apartment building in Marmande. He used to see my mother, brother, and me coming and going, and had some idea of what we had experienced during the war. He took a particular interest in me, offering to show me his stamp collection. I was fascinated with all his stamps which he kept neatly organized in his leather albums. He would explain to me what each stamp commemorated—what kings they portrayed, what battles, and so forth. In that way I learned a lot about French and European history. It was a way for me to acquire the knowledge that I might otherwise have received in school, which I had no interest in. But I had a great interest in stamps. He was so kind to me, in a fatherly way. He was almost like a substitute father. Other French kids collected stamps as well. It was a very popular hobby. I remember one day he asked me if I'd like to start my own collection, and I answered him positively and with great enthusiasm. He gave me a few stamps which became the foundation of my own collection. I kept up this hobby for many years and it includes both European and US stamps. I now keep my collection in a bank vault and hope that someday someone else will continue to build on what I started. What is most important to me about this episode is the love and patience that a Christian neighbor showed me. I will always remember Monsieur Blancher.

* * *

Finally, my mother received all the necessary paperwork for us to immigrate to the United States. Once we had our documents and our tickets, this was all I could think about. I knew I would miss my friend Claude Radzinsky, but I would not miss France to any measurable degree. Claude and I talked about our individual plans. I shared with him my excitement about going to America. He was preparing for entrance into the University of Paris. He eventually became a well-known engineer. We stayed in touch with each other for many years. He admirably succeeded in his career goal, building high-rise buildings and other engineering projects in many cities in Europe and the Middle East.

As a teenager, I had a very narrow view of the world, but I did know something about America. I had seen American movies, and everything about the United States intrigued me—its cities, its cars, its open spaces, its philosophy, and the freedom that people seemingly enjoyed without the fear of despots and anti-

Semites. For a rebellious teenager like me, I felt instinctively that America was where I belonged. I could hardly wait to leave France. I felt like a racehorse at the starting gate. I thought I could forget about the tribulations of my past and make something of myself in America, where I could become more than a scared little boy, more than a tailor's apprentice, and more than a rebellious teenager.

Reunited with my mother. I am seated on a motorcycle
and my brother Herbert is behind me.

Dressed in our Boy Scout uniforms, 1948, about to go on a bicycle trip.

(L-R) Herbert, Claude Radzinsky, my best friend, and me.

My mother's French residence card valid 1948-58.

My Federation Française de Cyclo-Tourisme membership card valid until 1950.

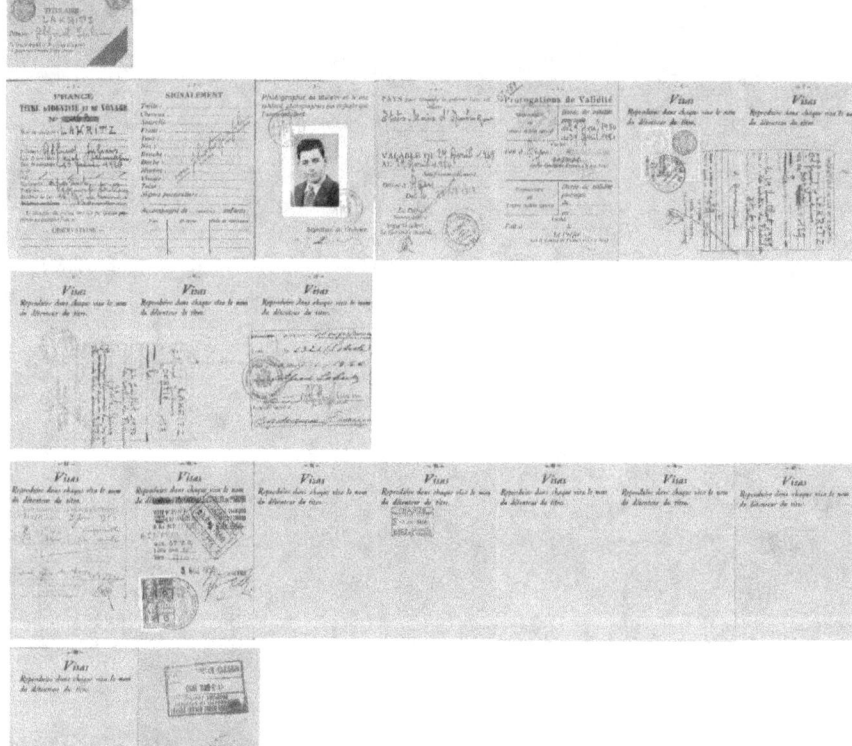

My exit visa to the United States stamped April 29, 1950 – April 29, 1951.
It lists my profession as "tailor's apprentice."

CHAPTER 11

Where Are You Going?

My mother was in constant contact with her uncle and my great-uncle, Max Fass, sending letters and occasional telegrams to California. My uncle and great-uncle used to send us money and care packages. I was introduced to American food, like peanut butter, that way. Every package gave me the belief that our immigration was eventually going to happen. It gave me hope.

But I had to be patient.

The Displaced Persons Act was signed into law by President Harry Truman in June 1948, enabling the United States to accept up to 200,000 refugees from European countries who had been affected by the war. Truman cited numerous clauses in the Act that he deemed unjust and discriminatory, and it was with great reluctance that he signed the Act:

> …The bad points of the bill are numerous. Together they form a pattern of discrimination and intolerance wholly inconsistent with the American sense of justice….The bill discriminates in callous fashion against displaced persons

of the Jewish faith....The bill also excludes many displaced persons of the Catholic faith who deserve admission....[19]

It took five years to obtain our visa. If you ask me, that was five years longer than it should have taken. And it was nearly fifteen years since the Germans had denied our first exit visa in Hamburg because my observant father refused to carry money on the Sabbath. (Looking back, I am sure God would have forgiven him if he had paid for the exit visa.)

The American relief organization that acted on behalf of my mother, brother, and me was the Hebrew Immigration Aid Society (HIAS), headquartered in New York City with a network of offices throughout Europe. It was established to assist displaced persons wishing to immigrate to the United States. HIAS gave my mother money, and it might even have paid for some of our travel expenses. As a precondition for coming to the United States, refugees had to show that they had some sort of sponsorship and some means to earn a living. In my mother's case, she declared herself a seamstress, and I was designated a tailor. The Fass family was our sponsor.[20]

---

[19] https://www.presidency.ucsb.edu/documents/statement-the-president-upon-signing-the-displaced-persons-act

[20] Founded as the Hebrew Immigrant Aid Society in 1881 to assist Jews fleeing pogroms in Russia and eastern Europe, HIAS has touched the life of nearly every Jewish family in America. From its beginnings in a storefront on the Lower East Side of Manhattan, a group of American Jews organized to provide much-needed comfort and aid to thousands of Jews fleeing waves of anti-Semitic riots. While those who arrived were refugees—people who were being killed in their homelands because of who they were— the world did not yet have a legal concept for people who needed safe refuge outside their homelands. HIAS established a bureau on Ellis Island in 1904, providing translation services, guiding immigrants through medical screenings, arguing before the Boards of Special Inquiry to prevent deportations, and obtaining bonds to guarantee employable status. HIAS lent some the $25 landing fee and sold railroad tickets at reduced rates to those headed for other cities. It even installed a kosher kitchen, which provided more than half a million meals to new arrivals on Ellis Island. The outbreak of World War I brought the largest influx of Jews from eastern Europe yet; more than 138,000 in that year alone. But soon after, restrictions limited the number of

Before we left Marmande, we bid a tearful *adieu* to the Ros family and to others who had shown us so much kindness. My mother kept in touch with the Ros family for many years afterwards, and likely with Madame Radzinsky as well.

I don't know how long it took us to pack. We didn't have much in the way of belongings, even after living in Marmande for five years. Other than some clothes, we probably gave our other possessions away, knowing that we would be able to replace household goods once we were settled in the United States.

My visa was stamped April 29, 1950, which I assume is the day that my mother, Herbert, and I left France. But before we left, my mother insisted that we go to Paris. She had never been, and she wanted to see the beauty of the city for herself. As a seamstress, she might even have wanted to look at the women's clothes designed by some of the famous designers such as Chanel and Dior.

While we were in the City of Light, we found the replica of the Statue of Liberty. From there we were sent to Rome by HIAS to await our transport to the United States. We stayed outside Rome and we were housed near a synagogue on the grounds of a film studio in an area called Cinecittà. There were other Jewish refugees housed there.

They were making a movie—*Quo Vadis*—which was set in ancient Rome. I was completely fascinated by what was going on and used to visit the set every day watching the actors perform

immigrants allowed into America to no more than two percent of the total of each nationality residing in the U.S. in 1890, severely restricting the entry of Jews from eastern Europe. Though precious few refugees were rescued during World War II due to the restrictive National Origins Act of 1924, HIAS provided immigration and refugee services to those who were. After the war, HIAS was instrumental in evacuating the displaced persons camps in Europe and aiding in the resettlement of some 150,000 people to 330 communities in the U.S., as well as Canada, Australia, and South America. In 1948, Israel was established as the Jewish homeland.

and seeing the sets moved around. In the movie, a common commander falls in love with a Christian hostage, and somehow that inspires him to rebel against Emperor Nero. I have no idea if the movie was good, but the people in the studio were nice to me. Having lived through so much deprivation, the idea of creating something—purely for the fun of it—held tremendous appeal for me. I knew that Hollywood was more or less near Oakland, where the Fass family lived, so that movie set was, in a way, an introduction to my new home.

As it turned out, *Quo Vadis* (which is Latin for "Where are you going?") was no ordinary movie. Strangely enough, the history of its production mirrors my own history. It was supposed to have been shot in the 1930s—just as I was supposed to have left Germany in the 1930s—but was postponed because of the war. Once it got back on track, MGM Studios built the most extensive collection of sets ever constructed for a movie shoot about eight miles from the center of Rome. The $7 million production included major stars—Deborah Kerr, Robert Taylor, and Peter Ustinov—thousands of extras, and even animals.

Filming started in May 1950, just at the time that we arrived in Rome. My mother met a German couple by the name of Hoenig who were related to a famous filmmaker in the United States, and they were staying on the grounds of the studio as were we. They were going to Hollywood to reunite with their relatives there. As I recall, they didn't have children and showed an interest not only in my mother but in my brother and me.

It was fabulous being in Rome and seeing the ancient buildings and Roman ruins, in addition to the fantasy history of the movie set. We were there for several weeks and toured the city. You can only imagine how excited I was to see another big city. Before going to Paris and staying in Rome, the largest cities I had any memory of were Lourdes and Marmande. (I think I was too young to have any vivid recollections of Kiel.) Now I was free to go where I wanted to without the threat of Nazis, bombs, and guns. I was free at last!

On the ocean liner to America, I became terribly seasick. My mother took the rough waters better. There were some calm days when we could wander the ship and speak to the passengers. Everyone was very nice to us. I spoke with a German engineer. He had gone to school in Germany, and he was not Jewish. He had great empathy for me and wanted to know what had happened to me during the war. He expressed his sincere sympathy for what my family and I had gone through. He acted like a big brother to me. He taught me how to shave. He was a pleasant, good person. When I asked him how long it took him to get a visa to come to the United States, he told me six months. The reason his visa application was accelerated is that he had a skill—engineers were in high demand in the United States. He might also have been living in one of the Displaced Persons Camps that were gradually being closed by the Allied nations, and it was incumbent upon the United States to find places for these people whenever possible.

When our ship sailed into the New York Harbor and I saw the Statue of Liberty, I cried. I cried because it seemed so momentous. I never thought I would see it, especially after so many years and so many false starts and dashed hopes. I cried, too, because it meant safety. We had traveled hundreds of miles across Europe, facing and evading danger at every turn. When we sailed into New York Harbor, we did so knowing that no invading army or navy would reach us. Even if we were Jewish, we were not in the crosshairs of a gun. We could, as the Emma Lazarus poem at the base of the Statue of Liberty promised, "breathe free."

I also knew that the Statue of Liberty represented the best of French culture and was a gift from the French people to the people of the United States. She was called *La Liberté éclairant le monde*: "Liberty Enlightening the World." In one hand she held a torch, and in the other, a book with the date of the signing of the Declaration of Independence, a symbol of the same values that had driven the French Revolution: liberty, equality, fraternity. In a strange way, she made America feel more welcoming to me.

As we were going through immigration, the officers made my mother swear that she was not entering the United States to kill the president, and that she was able to support herself. What indignities. My mother already had all the necessary documentation from the Fass family proving that we had reliable sponsors, and as for the issue of targeting the president, how many other immigrants were asked this same absurd question?

We arrived in New York City and were welcomed by my mother's cousin, Frieda Knecht, who lived in Brooklyn. Her husband was a taxi driver. They generously offered to have us stay with them in their apartment. That first day I made two enormous discoveries. I had to go to the bathroom, and so my cousin took me into a bar, where I saw the staff making frosties. I couldn't believe how phenomenal it was with its creamy smoothness (French ice cream was very icy). Then I discovered a jukebox. I was just amazed to see how it worked. I had never seen anything like it.

We stayed in Brooklyn for about two weeks. I was amazed at how much food my cousins ate. We had subsisted on very little during the war years, and even afterwards, we didn't have a lot of money to spend on food. The Knechts looked very fat to me, or maybe we looked very skinny to them. Perhaps both are true.

Many immigrants, of course, arrived in New York and settled there with the assistance of HIAS and relatives living in and around the city where there was a large Jewish population. But we had a home waiting for us on the West Coast, with an entire continent between us. After so many years moving from place to place, the idea of moving yet again didn't faze me. It probably should have. The North American continent was vast and diverse, and I knew very little of it. But I did know that every mile we traveled was contained within United States territory. We had no more borders to cross and no more visas to secure.

Even with the books the US Embassy had sent me, I could still speak only a few words of English. I had never had anyone to practice with. Access to English-language entertainment was scarce. (English-language films were banned by the Germans during the war.) I had seen a few American films that were dubbed in French, but I had not spent enough time watching them to pick up more than a few rudimentary words and phrases. A lot of them were Westerns, and the slang in those movies didn't do me much good. How was I going to make use of "Howdy, partner," or "Drop your gun?"

My mother, brother, and I had train tickets paid for by HIAS that took us from New York City to Oakland. It was a four-day trip. I remember looking out the window at the changing scenery—the farms, the mountains, and the deserts. I took everything in with an open mind. I felt like we were heading toward paradise, our salvation. There would be no more hate, no more horrors, no one chasing after us. At sixteen, I felt as if my life were just beginning.

On the train, a Black man gave us a menu in the dining car. (He was not the first Black person I had ever seen, but he was the first person of his race that I had ever spoken to. While we were in Paris, I saw many Black people who had come to France from the former French colonies.) I didn't know what I was reading on the menu because, of course, it was in English, but I finally picked a word that I knew. It was "corn." I knew this word because of the canned corned beef that Great-Uncle Max used to send us in care packages. When the waiter brought us what I had ordered, I was surprised. I thought it was going to be a corned beef sandwich.

I asked, "Is this our lunch?" He looked at us and was totally befuddled. What was sitting on our plates were cooked ears of corn—in France, corn is fed to the pigs and geese and not to people. But we were so hungry that I'm sure we ate whatever was on our plates. The train ride was magnificent. I thought of the train rides I had taken before and during the war. Each one was an escape from something—from the Nazis in Kiel, from the advancing German forces in Antwerp, from whatever police force was closing in on us. This time, we were traveling *to* something. And we saw our new country flashing by us out the train window. By the time we reached Oakland, I fully knew what corn was, and I was already feeling at home.

* * *

Today there are only faint traces of my family's time in Marmande. We were always transients—always refugees. We never owned property. Our name might appear on a tax roll or in a school roster buried in the archives of the town hall, but that's about it. Except for one thing.

The city of Marmande recognized my father's contributions to the Resistance effort. Shortly after the war, they declared him a hero of the war.

The city erected a monument recognizing those brave men and women who risked their lives under the cover of night. And there, on the base with a handful of other names, is the name "Sim Lakritz." The French misspelled my father's first name, Simche. It is the only Jewish name on the statue. It is the only indication that our family, once four people and then three, lived in Marmande and Saint-Pardoux. I would one day go back to Marmande and Saint-Pardoux to thank the people who saved my mother, took care of her during the darkest hours of the war, and sheltered her while her two sons were in the arms of strangers.

CHAPTER 12

"Vote for Lakritz—
Here's a Ritz!"

After fourteen years, a world war, the Holocaust, and personal tragedies, my mother, brother, and I arrived in the city of Oakland, California, joyously greeted by the Fass family, our family.

I don't remember culture shock or disorientation. I think I had moved around enough that I took the change in stride. What mattered most to me was the fact that my mother and brother were safe. No language barrier, financial hardship, or wrong turns in Oakland could ever compare with the traumas we had endured.

Oakland was across the Bay Bridge from San Francisco. Like Kiel, it was a port city, except that it faced the Pacific Ocean, not the Baltic Sea. In 1950 its population was very diverse, with people of many different ethnic and religious backgrounds, including large Chinese and Japanese populations—people whom I had never encountered in Europe. It was a blue-collar city, with men who worked at the port and shipyards. It was also in a region with outstanding institutions of higher learning, museums, restaurants, public parks, and fancy hotels. All of it was so different from the small towns of Saint-Pardoux, Marmande, Lourdes, Évian, and Tarbes, where I lived and hid during the war years.

In Oakland there were no overt signs of war. It amazed me that while European cities and towns had suffered great physical damage, America seemed to be a land untouched by the war, even if it was American military power and know-how that had contributed to the Allied victories against the Axis despots. I did not know if its citizens had been subject to rations, to gas shortages, or scarce food. To me, everything seemed thriving. It would only be later that I learned about the direct and indirect effects of World War II on its economy and people, and some of the ways that anti-Semites fueled hatred against the Jews even in idyllic America.

For the first few months, the three of us lived in one room of my uncle Michael Fass's three-bedroom house in Oakland on Pearl Street. It was a typical two-story wood-and-plaster type of home, with a porch in the front. They made room for us. Herb and I slept in one bed, and on the opposite side of the bedroom was one of their sons—either Jack or Eddie.

My uncle Michael Fass—my mother's brother—and his wife, my aunt Ida, were very religious Jews, and Ida was a fantastic kosher cook. My cousins Eddie and Jack were older than Herb and me. They had gone to Oakland Technical High School. Eddie was very outgoing and had been the Bulldog mascot at Oakland Tech. Their sister, Sally, had gone to an even better school: Oakland High School.

The entire Fass family welcomed us; we never felt like outsiders, and we were never made to feel like we were imposing upon them. They knew quite a bit about what we had gone through during the war, and my great-uncle had letters from my father, early on when we were turned over to the summer camp. That fact alone was evidence of the hardship that we had endured, and of course they learned more directly from my mother, but those stories were kept from my brother and me for a long time.

Many other Jewish refugees who had come to the United States were not so lucky as to have receptive and compassionate relatives waiting there for them. Many upper-class Jews looked down their noses at their Jewish immigrant relatives, who arrived without a dime in their pockets, wearing strange clothes, and speaking what little English they might have known with strange accents. These Jewish immigrants—many of whom had been deported to concentration camps, had lived in ghettos, had been slave laborers to their Nazi captors—kept quiet about the tragedies they had lived through. What was the point of talking about what they had witnessed? There was a code of silence, especially when it came to sharing their stories with their children. Why upset them? The reality of what had happened seeped out slowly with the publication of memoirs such as Elie Wiesel's *Night* (1960), Primo Levi's *If This Is a Man* (1947), and Viktor Frankl's *Man's Search for Meaning* (1946), which became popular long after they were originally published. Early readers found their contents hard to accept as the truth. And perhaps the most famous of early Holocaust books is *The Diary of a Young Girl*, composed of journal entries written by Anne Frank, which was published in Dutch in 1947 and then in English and many other languages in 1953.

For the first time since we left Kiel, we finally experienced a full Jewish family life. The Fasses belonged to Beth Abraham Synagogue, a Conservative congregation. We joined them. The chief officiant was Rabbi Harold M. Schulweis, who would later move to Los Angeles and become the head of Valley Beth Shalom Synagogue in Encino, a neighborhood with a significant Jewish population. He was a great leader of the Jewish community and was revered by his congregants. Rabbi Schulweis became a widely published author of spiritual philosophy.[21] He would become an important counselor to me as I entered college and beyond.

My mother supported us with the same skills she used to support us in France: sewing. She got a job fitting women's clothing at I. Magnin & Company, a fancy Jewish-owned department store in San Francisco. Every day she took the bus from Oakland across the Bay Bridge and fitted clothing purchased at the store by San Francisco's high society and tourists who visited the city. Back then, the whole Bay Area was industrial. But San Francisco, just as it does now, had serious money. Many descendants of the original Jewish settlers who came to California during the gold rush from New York and from abroad—people like Levi Strauss, who supplied gear to the 1850s gold miners— still lived in San Francisco and patronized I. Magnin. My mother's salary was augmented by the money she received from the French government—a pension tied to the fact that my father had been declared a hero of the Resistance. She continued to collect it even though she no longer lived in France.

[21]His writings include *Evil and the Morality of God* (1983); *In God's Mirror: Reflections and Essays* (1990); *For Those Who Can't Believe: Overcoming the Obstacles to Faith* (1994); *Meditations and Prayers for the Renewal of the Body and the Renewal of the Spirit* (2000); *Finding Each Other in Judaism: Meditations on the Rites of Passage from Birth to Immortality* (2001); *When You Lie Down and When You Rise Up: Nightstand Meditations* (2001); and *Conscience: The Duty to Obey and the Duty to Disobey* (2008).

My mother had changed her name from Marjem (her birth name) to Mariam or Marie while living in France. In Oakland, she became Mary Lakritz. My mother was very practical and smart, and I think she anglicized her name to make it easy for her customers to ask for her. And in some ways, it might have been a way for her to "fit in" and to leave behind all the painful memories of her past. This is speculation on my part because, like so many other things, we rarely talked about this. I just accepted that this was the right thing to do. I admired my mother for her practical mind, her loving kindness, and her courage. And at about that time, I changed my middle name from Julius to Julien, the French spelling of Julian. I have kept that name ever since, but with my middle initial being "J" it can stand for either name.

Once my mother started making a decent income, we moved out of the Fass family house and into an apartment a few doors away on Harrison Street. It was a small ground-floor unit. Upstairs was a crazy neighbor who liked to sing. Herb and I didn't appreciate that sort of entertainment, so we often hung out at the Fass house, listening to the radio. Eventually they got a television, and we went over to watch wrestling matches.

I felt right at home in the United States in a way I never had in France. Perhaps it was because I'd felt like a refugee in France, living there under duress and enduring the traumas of separation, poverty, and of course my father's death. I also found that the America I lived in felt a lot like the America I had seen in movies. Or maybe it was my imagination. Either way, I was comfortable. And most importantly, I assumed, correctly, that the United States would become my permanent home.

My most immediate challenge concerned school. I was ill-prepared for my grade level. And I still struggled with English, as

French was my first language. I had long ago forgotten whatever German I had once known.

As I mentioned before, I attended *un école laïque* in Marmande for a short time, a nonsectarian school. I didn't enjoy school, and I didn't pay much attention when I attended. Even when I did, though, the French education system didn't enable me to learn much.

You'd have thought that teachers in the nonsectarian school would have been relatively lax. Nothing could have been further from the truth. My teachers would call students up to the blackboard and make them write the same thing over and over again if they made a mistake, just to humiliate them. They held on to rulers and, if they decided that a student had broken a rule or done poorly, they would make the student clasp his hands and then both hands would get whacked with the ruler. Corporal punishment was accompanied by all sorts of put-downs and derision. And it wasn't because I was Jewish. All students were targeted.

And forget about the academic lessons. They were too structured, with no explanations or adaptation. You just had to follow along at their pace and remember whatever you could. For me, it usually wasn't much. Even then, I was well aware that I knew nothing—but I wanted to learn. I suppose I had learned a great deal in my personal trials. But I was completely ignorant of structured academic learning.

I enrolled in Oakland Technical High School, which Eddie and Jack Fass attended. I started in tenth grade at age sixteen. Though my brother was almost a year younger, he entered the same grade. Up to that point, he had always been stronger in school than I was, so he was better prepared. He had taken his studies seriously in France, whereas I had no patience for what was happening in school, and as I have mentioned before, I abandoned my classes and worked as a tailor's assistant as soon as it was legal to do so. Whatever I learned, I learned in the tailor shop or on the streets. I was a scrappy kid, honing my survival skills. The only places where I really felt as if I received valuable knowledge was in the Boy Scouts and with Dr. Landau, my Hebrew teacher from Agen. I wanted to make him proud of me.

Initially, American education seemed like a joke. As much as I had disliked French education, I didn't understand the American teaching style at all. It was too liberal. The teachers constantly wanted students to share their own opinions and come up with their own answers. I thought, "Shouldn't the teachers be giving us information? What is the point of having students express their opinions? How can we have opinions if we don't know anything yet?"

I came to understand that sharing opinions was part of the educational process. When we shared opinions, teachers provided us with facts and ideas to influence or complement those opinions, and then our opinions adapted to the facts. I remember very little of those classroom discussions, but I do remember that I participated enthusiastically. I had no social standing anyway, so I had no reason to be embarrassed if I made any strange or naive comments—and I'm sure I had strong opinions!

Before long, I expressed my opinions in nearly fluent English.

When I entered high school, I had spoken practically no English. At first, I am sure it was not easy for our teachers, but our language difficulties inspired great compassion, tolerance, and patience among the teachers and even the students. I don't remember ever being made fun of.

But even early on, I was so motivated and so in love with America that I embraced English wholeheartedly. I was deeply motivated to fit in, and fitting in required that I learn English. I probably drew on my previous mastery of languages. My partial knowledge of German had quickly turned into fluency in French, and French gave way to English almost as easily. I was completely fluent in English in six months. I never did lose my French, though, and I spoke English with an accent in high school. Predictably, my nickname became "Frenchie." At first, it was kind of a put-down. But I got used to it, and as the other kids got to know me, it became endearing. And most importantly, I never heard anyone make fun of me because I was Jewish or call me bad names. I felt elated to be accepted for who I was without derision, criticism, or punishment. Eventually I lost my French accent when speaking English. This is something I am very proud of.

I dove into life at Oakland Tech, literally, by joining the swim team. My years of summer camp and Boy Scouts developed in me a love for the water. I had learned to swim in the Garonne River, which originated in the city of Bordeaux and passed through Lourdes. I don't think any other guy on the team could say that! My best event was the breaststroke, and I won a few swim meets in high school.

I acclimated to American culture quickly—so quickly, in fact, that I joined the yell team and made my way to assistant yell leader and then to yell leader, cheering on the Bulldogs of Oakland Tech. It wasn't hard to be enthusiastic. I cherished my new home and new school, and I enjoyed cheering on its teams. I became what we would have called back then a "big man on campus." I went to school dances and had plenty of dates, too. I felt as if I had been reborn, shedding all the weight of my previous life that was filled with sadness and pain. I now felt joy and excitement and a desire to learn and to be popular. And I was.

My mentor on the yell team was Hank MacDonald. He was tremendously talented and energetic. I became one of his assistants, along with an Italian-born boy, a Japanese-born girl, and a Protestant girl. I had a diverse group of friends outside the team, too. One of my best friends was a Mormon boy. I befriended several Black students. My high school reflected the diversity of the Oakland population, and it was liberating to learn with and befriend students of many different backgrounds. I don't remember if there was a large Jewish cohort at Oakland Tech, but if there was, there was no need for me to stay within the confines of that group. I was accepted by everyone and was an enthusiastic joiner.

Then I ran for head yell leader. That was a schoolwide election. We would go around the high school with boxes of Ritz crackers and yell, "Vote for Lakritz—here's a Ritz!" and hand out crackers to whomever would take them. I won that election and was installed as head yell leader during basketball season of eleventh grade. I didn't get to choose my assistant yell leaders, but Herb tried out and became one, along with a few other students.

Being head yell leader meant that I was also on the student council. I loved it. In addition to our official duties, student council members had standing permission to cut class for "important student council business." I used that a few times. After experiencing the freedom of my boyhood in France, running around on the streets or working in the tailor shop, I was glad to slip away from the strict schedule of American high school. The freedom I experienced in the United States is one of the aspects of my new life that I treasured most during my high school years. I greeted each day with enthusiasm and a sense of well-being and happiness, embracing each new adventure that came my way.

Looking back on this time, it's hard to believe that I transitioned so easily from a teenager who barely spoke a word of English to head yell leader, learning all the cheers and prompting the fans to sing and yell the praises of our various teams at Oakland Tech. I was so determined and dedicated, and these qualities ensured that I would get ahead and succeed—and I did!

One of my outstanding experiences in high school was attending a speech by President Harry S. Truman. His words were inspirational. I also learned that his best friend during his thirties was a Jewish haberdasher. The two men became fast friends, and Truman was influenced by him. Their friendship may have promoted his tolerant attitude toward the Jews and his criticism of the Displaced Persons Act, which he reluctantly signed. He felt that it didn't go far enough in opening the doors of the United States to the many eastern European Jews who had suffered so mightily against the cruel and barbaric hands of the Nazis.

I had a lot of help with my high school studies. My French teacher was extremely supportive, and I also had help from interns at the University of California at Berkeley, who were education students and were assigned to work with us to improve our English. French was one of my favorite classes, for obvious reasons, and I enjoyed philosophy, too. The two classes had a lot in common, especially since many great philosophers were French. It seemed familiar to me.

I couldn't believe how invested people were in my success here in the United States. They willingly volunteered to tutor me to ensure that I would get ahead. I don't know why they were so nice to me, but they were, and I will be forever grateful for their aid.

* * *

During the summers and weekends, I worked for my great-uncle Max or Uncle Michael in their junkyards. They were in the recycling business just as my grandfather and father had been, but the money they made far exceeded what my family made in Kiel. I asked to be paid in silver coins because I knew that paper money in Germany and elsewhere during the war had become worthless. I don't know how I was so clever, but my uncle went along with my request. I didn't trust that a dollar would hold its value. It's funny thinking about it now, but back then, I was convinced that one day a dollar—like money printed by the Vichy government— would become worthless. And of course, inflation was rampant throughout western Europe after the war. Prices for the most rudimentary goods made most things out of reach. I was not convinced yet that such a thing would not happen in the United States. Like my accent, this was a vestige of my youth. It can take a long time for old fears to dissipate; in fact, some never do.

At some point I got a job as a stock boy in a local grocery store to contribute to the household income. The job was ordinary but fun. I enjoyed chatting with customers, and I saw it as yet another way to get to know Oakland and try out my charm on people. But there was more to the job than that. The grocery store had a raffle, and the prize was two round-trip tickets to New York sponsored by Pan American Airways. In order to qualify for the raffle, you had to guess how many air miles Pan Am flew. I guessed a high number and Herb guessed a low number. And guess who won? Herb did.

Herb and I went to New York. It was our only major trip out of the Bay Area. Ironically, of all the destinations Pan Am could have taken us to, we returned to the one other American city we had previously visited. It was still a thrill. We were treated like princes by the airline and toured the city. By that time, my English was good enough to handle whatever came our way during the trip. Our mother stayed home. I'm sure she was delighted for us, but I'm also sure that she worried about her two sons wandering around a strange city. At least she was comforted in the knowledge that Pan Am was watching out for us. This would be the first of numerous trips I would eventually take to satisfy my curiosity about the world, and in some cases, search for the truth of my past.

The only sad note in my otherwise happy teenage years was the recognition that my mother carried around so much pain in her heart from the loss of her beloved husband, my father. She hardly talked about him until many years later when I asked her some carefully thought-out questions. She had a box of documents and photographs that she carried with her through the war and brought to the United States. She and I sat down and went through this box, which included the postcard signed by my father.

It was then, so many years after I had waved goodbye at the train station, that I read his final word, "*Adjeu.*"

CHAPTER 13

May Justice Be Served

I did well at Oakland Tech. I loved chemistry. I was amazed that you could make something new by combining two elements together. It was a great time of discovery for me. I didn't like math, though.

I attended school with a lot of Black and Asian kids, which was certainly not the case when I was living in Marmande. One of the kids in my school was John Brodie, who went on to Stanford University and then played for the San Francisco 49ers. I made many deep friendships in high school. I was treated as an equal by my classmates and flourished in this environment.

I graduated Oakland Tech in 1953 when I was nineteen years old. It was a very proud moment for me. Just a few years earlier, I was a teenager who spoke no English and barely had any substantial schooling to speak of. My mother was proud of me. But there would be more *naches* to come for her to smile about. Anything I could accomplish that made her happy made me happy. I owe her my life, and I will never take that for granted.

In my opinion, the ultimate goal of almost any high school kid in California is to go to college at the University of California at Berkeley, which was just a few miles from our apartment on Harrison Street in Oakland. But I didn't have the grades, so I started college across the bay at San Francisco State University.

I worked hard and got a B+ average in my first semester. That was enough to get me admitted as a transfer student to UC Berkeley. Herb and I were in the same class at Berkeley because he was admitted immediately after his senior year in high school.

I likened being accepted into UC Berkeley to the sky opening up and God giving me this unbelievable opportunity—something I could not have imagined until I came to the United States and observed the opportunities that other students were being given. Up to this point, almost everything my mother, brother, and I had done was in the name of survival. The idea of improving our lives and chasing dreams was still hard to fathom. But UC Berkeley represented a whole new set of opportunities. I became an equal to all the other students. I was in the midst of greatness—people who had helped invent the computer, the hydrogen bomb, modern medicine, and all the rest.

Studying at Berkeley enabled me to seriously consider and formulate my long-term career goals in a way that I never could have imagined when we were scraping by in France. Since I majored in economics and did very well, I could easily have gone into business, but making money was never in and of itself a motivating factor in my life. I was exposed to people who ran their own businesses, such as the Fasses, and I had worked alongside people in retail sales, but these ventures did not attract my attention. I realized that what I wanted to do more than anything else was to become a lawyer. I had a debate with myself and realized that what I valued most was protecting people from persecution, helping to guarantee people the liberties they were entitled to.

My mistreatment in France was one of the motivations for setting my sights on the law. I resolved to pursue a legal career so that I could ensure equitable treatment through the law. I learned what a precious jewel justice is, and what a travesty life is without its protection. I had suffered greatly as a Jew in France, and the experiences I had growing up and being persecuted for being a Jew instilled in me the desire to protect others from injustice. I believed that becoming a lawyer would fulfill this desire. Once I made up my mind, nothing stopped me from pursuing this dream.

To prepare myself for law school, I took a wide selection of undergraduate courses. In literature I read Shakespeare, contemplating the moral ambiguities in his plays. In French literature I read poets like Baudelaire. I took philosophy and was totally engrossed. I remember I was having difficulty with an assignment in philosophy class, and I spoke with Rabbi Schulweis, who helped me to organize my thoughts. I think the topic was on the progression of ideas—I envisioned a ladder that I climbed from one concept to the next. Rabbi Schulweis was so generous with his time for me, a Berkeley student with an inquisitive and restless mind. In fact, he was instrumental in getting me into Berkeley, so he might have felt that he had a stake in my excelling there.

I majored in economics and remembered learning how President Franklin D. Roosevelt brought the country out of the Great Depression. (Maybe by then I had learned the value of a dollar and didn't need to be paid in silver.) I took practical classes like accounting. I even took geology and absolutely loved it, probably because of all my adventures in the outdoors with the French Boy Scouts and even earlier on the hikes with the OSE.

Even with all my academic pursuits and social activities, I wanted to help my mom by working part-time and to cover my out-of-pocket costs at Berkeley. I received a scholarship to attend Berkeley, but there were still some costs with matriculating there, such as books, joining a fraternity, and the like.

For a while on Saturdays and Sundays I washed dishes at a hamburger stand in Berkeley for two Catholic ladies who absolutely loved me. For whatever reason, washing dishes didn't bother me, and I guess the ladies appreciated my sunny demeanor. The work was tiring, and I was coated in grease by the end of a shift. But for whatever reason, I enjoyed it.

I also gained freedom in the most American way possible: I bought a car.

It was a used 1939 Chevrolet with side running boards. I probably paid $350 for the car, which was more than it was worth. But it was in very good condition. It had been owned by an older woman, the salesman said. Maybe this was a routine white lie, but I had a feeling that he really wanted me to think that I got a good car and that it was safe and that it was in good condition, and that I didn't get taken advantage of. Truthfully, I knew next to nothing about cars, but it ran just fine and got me around. It was the first car that my family ever owned, and I drove my mother around when she needed to run errands from time to time, sparing her a bus ride from Oakland into San Francisco.

I also got a part-time job at Campbell's Department Store. I was a stock boy in the china department, and I loved unloading and sorting all the crystal and china. It was all charming to me. I never felt jealous of the wealthy customers; I was so grateful to be safe, well-fed, earning a few dollars, and close to my mother and my brother.

I had fun at Berkeley, too.

I joined a Jewish fraternity, Sigma Alpha Mu, known as "Sammy." It was a very upper-middle-class, intellectual fraternity. After living so much of my life as an outcast, the feeling of being someplace where I was surrounded by people who appreciated me and didn't discriminate against me was indescribable. They accepted Herb and me, even though at first we lived with our mother because we couldn't afford to live in the fraternity house (though we eventually did). I loved fraternity life, and I even ran for president. I lost to Marv Cohen, but I'm glad I had the guts to run. I think I knew even back then that when I became a lawyer, I would sometimes win and sometimes lose. Losing is okay as long as you work even harder for the next win and you did your best to represent your client. In my case, I lost to a true genius. Marv graduated from Berkeley, entered the field of theoretical physics, became a professor at Berkeley—and went on to win the National Medal of Science!

Throughout my undergraduate years at Berkeley, my studies always came first. I wanted to make the most of the amazing opportunity I had been given. I wanted to take full advantage of every hour that I spent on the Berkeley campus. The fraternity house was usually too noisy for studying. I found a special place in the library—a desk and a chair in a distant corner with just enough light—and I used to study there for hours on end. I wanted to get the best grades possible so that I could earn a spot in law school.

At least once, though, I ended up somewhere I hadn't planned to be.

* * *

For a while, the city's major newspaper, the *San Francisco Chronicle,* ran the Hunt for Emperor Norton's Prize. The *Chronicle* ran the "hunt" for about a decade from 1953 to 1962.

Every day, over the course of a few weeks, the newspaper published a clue in its pages that pointed to the location of a prize. The clues led to a bronze medallion buried somewhere in San Francisco. The medallion was shaped like a star with "1953" embossed on it to commemorate the first year of the hunt. It was struck by the jeweler Shreve & Co., which was founded during the gold rush and was a well-known jeweler and gold and silver trader. Whoever found the medallion was to bring it to the *Chronicle*'s office and receive a reward of $1,000 in silver dollars.

It was basically the perfect invitation to get an entire fraternity in trouble. At some point during the hunt, a Sammy brother thought he had figured out where the medallion was buried. He directed us to a park alongside a freeway and, within the park, to a small lake. We all brought shovels and excavated like crazy to find the treasure.

All of a sudden, the whole lake was surrounded by police cars. "Raise your hands!" we heard over a loudspeaker. "This is the Berkeley police!" Not exactly what Emperor Norton promised us. The police directed us to walk slowly away from where we were digging. Then they packed between twenty and thirty Sammy brothers into a van headed for the police precinct. I was scared to death. I had no idea what was going to happen or how serious our crime was.

We were put in separate cells, some of which held other inmates. They asked us what we were in for. When we told them it was for trespassing, they made fun of us. Hardened criminals, we were not.

Stan Gold was one of two lawyers assigned to help us. While discussing my case, Stan and I hit it off. He talked the court into letting my brother and me off. He explained to the police that we were not citizens of the United States yet and a criminal charge could hinder our petition for citizenship. For whatever reason, the judge decided that they'd gone far enough and heeded Stan's recommendation. He probably argued, "These boys have learned their lesson," and he got us off without a charge.

As it was, the cops were probably playing a trick on us—picking on dumb college kids on a slow night. But the incident stuck with me. I vowed never to put myself in a situation like that again. It also brought me into direct contact with the justice system. I imagined other accused criminals in the very same cells and was reminded of the millions of innocent people who were "convicted," sent to far more terrifying prisons, and sentenced to death by the Nazis. Our ill-fated quest for Emperor Norton's medallion was another reason I wanted to become a lawyer. To make sure that minor transgressions were not punished unjustly—that "the punishment fit the crime."

Stan Gold and I stayed in touch. A couple years later, I asked him for advice about law school. He encouraged me to apply and even sponsored my application. He was my inspiration. In truth, I probably hadn't even met a real lawyer before Stan. He made my ambition seem that much more real.

* * *

I think my mother was lonely when Herb and I went off to college, even though we were only a few miles away. She had her job to keep her busy, and she spent plenty of time with the Fasses. But I think she thought about finding someone to share her life with. Whether she ever imagined that she'd fall in love again was another matter.

A friend of hers introduced her to an immigrant living in San Francisco who had been a soldier in the French Foreign Legion. He served his military duties in Morocco. I didn't really like him because he wasn't very refined. I always believed my mother deserved sainthood for what she had done to save us during and after the war. This man was not her reward. However, he had a pension from his time in the French military. I suspected that he did not need to work, so he had time to give my mother the companionship she craved.

He proposed marriage and she accepted. I wasn't very happy about this, but I thought that he would bring her some modicum of happiness and financial stability beyond what her salary provided.

After a while, she realized that she had made a grave mistake. He was selfish and caused her a lot of pain. She shared her unhappiness with me, and together we decided that it would be best for her to get a divorce. She spoke with Stan Gold, and he offered to represent her in divorce proceedings, but she changed her mind and decided to stay married to him, for better or worse.

When she had a heart attack, she refused to have a pacemaker. The doctor told her that it would save her life, but she didn't think her life was worth living. By that time, I was working as a lawyer and Herb was struggling to establish his accounting practice. Ostensibly we "did not need her anymore"—or at least she saw things that way, which was far from the truth. Sadly, she died on September 28, 1970, at the age of seventy-five. It was one of the saddest days of my life. I felt as if an angel had left the earth. I only hoped that she might be reunited in the afterlife with my father, if there is an afterlife.

* * *

What were some of the other reasons that motivated me to go to law school after graduating from UC Berkeley? As I mentioned, one of the reasons was Stan Gold's encouragement and his example. I thought he was a brilliant person, and I wanted to follow in his footsteps. I admired greatly the way he argued our case to the judge and got us out of jail without jeopardizing our chances for US citizenship.

I became a naturalized citizen in 1954, as did my brother. I remember one of my co-workers at Campbell's Department Store drove me to the courthouse in downtown San Francisco for my official naturalization ceremony.

Another reason that I wanted to become a lawyer goes back to my early teenage years in Marmande. Every day when I passed the courthouse on my way to Monsieur Robert's tailor shop, I saw lawyers all dressed up in their black robes, wearing wigs, and looking to me like the most important men in the world. I thought to myself, "I want to do that someday." That thought might have been strange, since at the time I was stitching men's lapels. But of course, I saw what I was doing as temporary. I had big dreams for myself; I thought I was clever, and I believed in my innate intelligence, which I had not really put to good use up until that point. The idea of becoming a lawyer did not seem that unrealistic to me, given my self-assessment. Moreover, I was innately curious about the world and drawn to the concepts of good and evil and justice and injustice. I had experienced plenty of both during the war years. I thought that being a lawyer was the most prestigious career a smart person could aspire to. It amazes me now that I came to that conclusion at such a young age.

I was accepted to UC Berkeley Law School, which was ranked the Number 2 law school in the United States at the time. It is still consistently listed in the Top 14 law schools nationwide to this day and attracts an outstanding faculty.

Once I went to law school I learned about the precious jewel of justice. I took a class on equity with a professor who had studied at Harvard. Not only was he brilliant, but he had an engaging personality and a great sense of humor, and that made the subject come alive for me. From that moment on, I knew I was in the right place. Everything I had studied as an undergraduate made sense to me—whether it was the plays of Shakespeare or the poetry of Baudelaire. Looking at their words and thoughts through the lens of law gave everything I had studied a new dimension. I was hooked. Becoming a law student was a miracle. I strove with every bone in my body to study and do well.

The law suits my personality. I do not do well with ambiguity—I want to uncover the facts of a case and develop an argument supported by the truth. I believe it is essential to back up your opinion with facts, not "intuition" or inspiration or an educated guess. I crave research, digging into archives, and finding proof.

It is for these reasons that I began to look into what had happened to my family during the war—to the thirty-one relatives who were killed, and most importantly, to my father. Until I entered law school, I really knew almost nothing about my father's fate, about his death at Majdanek. Whatever my mother knew she did not share with me, and her box of collected documents offered no clues about his death.

I was intent upon unearthing everything I could to prove what happened to my father, and over time I was able to create a complete dossier with all the evidence necessary to say unequivocally and with absolute certainty when and where he died. My knowledge of legal research was put to use in researching the fate of my father and our relatives.

As painful as the truth was, it put to rest all the uncertainty that I had carried with me for so many years. I had to know what happened to him.

CHAPTER 14

A Satisfied Man

When I was a child, I experienced the great love and respect my mother and father had for each other. It was one of those marriages made in heaven, for lack of a better term. They shared many common interests, despite the fact that they were brought together by a matchmaker. I am sure if my father had not been killed, if they had been able to immigrate to the United States, they would have had a fulfilling and happy married life until they departed from this earth.

Unfortunately, in my mind, God abandoned my father in the darkest days of the war. I wonder what he thought as he was digging the trench at Majdanek; and I wonder what my mother thought as one day after another ticked by with no word from her beloved. This separation was only compounded by the separation from her two precious boys—Herbert and me.

With my parents as an example of love and sacrifice, I knew someday I would get married. I had the opportunity in high school and college to meet numerous attractive women, but no one turned my world upside until I met Judy Lenoff. We were brought together by sheer luck while I was in my second year of law school at Berkeley.

I had gone out to dinner with a group of friends, and nearby was the Hillel Student Union, where a party was in progress. We all decided to see what was cooking there. One of my fraternity brothers—he was actually my "little brother" in Sigma Alpha Mu—was chatting with two girls, one of whom was his girlfriend. I wasn't sure who the other girl was, but she was very cute and I made sure that he introduced me to her. She was a freshman at Berkeley and his girlfriend's friend. I found out later that she was originally from New York and had grown up in Los Angeles' San Fernando Valley, where she went to Birmingham High School at a time when the school was still housed in trailers to accommodate all the students who were the product of the population boom after World War II. Southern California was a magnet for the soldiers who had been stationed on the West Coast. When they compared their homes with the California lifestyle—with its great weather, its beaches, and its opportunities—they saw no reason to return to Kansas, or New York, or Pennsylvania. This population boom would fuel the economy of the state and provide demand for goods and services (like newly minted lawyers like me).

Judy and I hit it off immediately. It felt like a *coup de foudre*—a clap of thunder. Our first date was for coffee at the International House, and then we went to a party together. I recall that we made out, which back in the day might have been a little fast, but we were so attracted to each other. We dated for a while and then declared that we were in love, and this was it. We married on February 1, 1959, a month shy of our first date together a year earlier.

Judy voluntarily terminated her education at Berkeley to support us while I was finishing law school and then looking for a job. She went to secretarial school, which was not what she wanted to do, but her salary helped pay the bills. Many years later, after having our children, Judy went back to school to pursue her dream of becoming a nurse.

As a loving and supportive wife, she agreed to take a secretarial program as long as we would not have to live in Oakland after I graduated law school. I don't quite know why she wanted to move back to Los Angeles, but she made it clear that she didn't want to settle in Oakland. I had been offered a job as a personal injury attorney in San Francisco, but that did not interest me, and so it made sense for us to move even if my family was in Oakland and all my contacts were there. One of my friends even opined that I could have become a judge had I stayed in Oakland because of all my family contacts, but that idea falls into the category of "shoulda, woulda, coulda…"

Instead, we moved to Los Angeles and stayed with Judy's parents until we found our own apartment. Her father generously contributed $500 a month to help cover our living expenses and introduced me to one of his golfing buddies, who was a lawyer. He asked if they needed a bright young associate, and before I knew it, I had a position as a general practitioner.

Judy and I share so many common interests. We both love sports, hiking, and camping; we love to paint scenes of nature; we love to travel; we love to socialize; and we both love to learn. (Right now, Judy is taking an online French course. As I write this, I can hear her professor prompting her over Zoom.)

We also love being parents, which we didn't delay for very long after we married.

Our first child, Jennifer, was born on July 13, 1960, and our son, Gary, two years later, on June 8, 1962. Gary and his wife Alane have two daughters, Jessica and Sarah. Gary graduated from UCLA and then went to business school, worked in banking, and now runs his own company. Jennifer also went to UCLA. She worked in the entertainment industry on the creative side. She is married to Gary Salomons, an attorney, and they have two sons, Brian and Matthew.

I freely admit that I had my faults in raising our children. I strived to give them a sense of security—something that I lacked for many years—which is why this is so important to me. From time to time, I had bursts of anger if they misbehaved, but I worked hard to curtail these outbursts. (This reminds me a bit of my father's temperament.) My children may have some resentment toward my anger—especially my son, but he always knew that I loved him. Each child has two children of their own, so we are indulgent grandparents to four wonderful kids. Over the years we have taken the children on trips to Europe to expose them to cultural sites, wine, and food. And from time to time we have included visits to the places that were part of my childhood. Judy and I have also traveled without the children, and she is a marvelous companion, up for anything, and willing to indulge me in my desire to revisit the places where I was hidden and lived. Many of these trips stirred up intense emotions in me.

Judy and I also share a love of scouting. Over the years when our children were in scouting troops, Judy and I led troops on various adventures and guided them in achieving their badges, graduating from one level to the next. I was on the Girl Scout Council of San Fernando Vally for nine years. Judy was a Girl Scout leader and I used to go with her when she led her troop on expeditions. Scouting was the highlight of my childhood after the war, and I was delighted to pass along my love of scouting and nature to my children and share it with Judy.

I am proud to say that I have been a good provider. I have had a successful career as a lawyer. My personality is well suited to advocacy because I am a fighter. I can easily get fired up. When I am attacked by my legal opponent, I usually try to get in the last word in defense of my client. I am like a pit bull. I thrive on doing legal research to see where there is precedent, and this penchant for research has been put to good use in researching the history of my family. For every statement I have made in this book, I have the facts to back them up.

By becoming a lawyer, I found a way to protect people from injustice—the kind of injustice that I had suffered. I went into civil law and handled many cases over my almost fifty-year career. I was a general practitioner because I liked the variety. In my early years as an attorney, I worked for several law firms. I became an associate at Gepner & Fox, a downtown Los Angeles law firm that Judy's father introduced me to. For a while I worked for a solo practitioner at Schulman & Selwin, and he'd give me all the difficult cases. He desperately needed my help, which was great training for going out on my own. One of the cases I handled went down in the annals of California law for testing the laws of insanity. It is often used as legal precedent by lawyers today.

While I practiced law and after I retired, I did pro bono work as a mediator and arbitrator as a way of giving back for all the blessings I had in my career. I take pride in bringing people together to resolve a case. I used to tell the warring parties, "No one benefits from this." I always looked for a resolution.

One of my most difficult cases in which the lawyers on both sides thanked me was a dispute between two computer companies. The issue involved an employee who had left one company and stole the list of their clients and shared them with his new employer. The case involved millions of dollars. When I settled the case, both lawyers were grateful for the role I played as their mediator. Everyone involved recognized that if the case was not settled, they would end up in court. It's best to find a resolution to avoid the expenditure of time and money required for a trial.

I consider myself incredibly fortunate to have married a wonderful woman, to have two children who have given Judy and me the joy of parenthood and grandparenthood, and to have pursued a career in the law that has given me tremendous satisfaction.

I wonder—what would that rebellious teenager walking through the streets of Marmande think of his almost eighty-nine-year-old self living in a beautiful house overlooking the hills of San Fernando Valley, surrounded by the many mementos of his travels, his family, and his career? I think he would be amazed.

Aboard the ocean liner taking my mother, Herbert and me to the United States. I'm 16 years old and looking very spiffy in my outfit with white sneakers.

My brother Herbert and me graduating from the University of California, Berkeley in 1958, with my proud mother standing between us.

I insisted that my mother put on my cap and gown.

Judy Lenoff and me getting married on February 1, 1959,
at the Beverly Hilton Hotel.

Judy and me with our children and grandchildren. (L-R) Sarah Lakritz, granddaughter; my wife Judy; Jennifer Salomons, our daughter; Alane Lakritz, our son's wife; Jessica Lakritz, our granddaughter, Gary Lakritz, our son, Gary Salomons, our son-in-law; me; Matthew Salomons and Brian Salomons, our grandsons.

CHAPTER 15

Rites of Return

A few years ago, I went to an event at the French consulate in Los Angeles. I chatted briefly with the consul general and told him that I was a child of the Holocaust and had spent the majority of my childhood in France. He observed in a way that did not really surprise me, "I bet you never have nor will return."

After what happened to my mother, my brother, and me, he wondered how I could tolerate standing on the soil where my father was arrested and sent to his death and where I was scorned and ridiculed for being a Jew.

"No," I told him. "It is a beautiful country—what cheese, what wine, what art!"

The truth is that I am of two minds when I think about France. It is a country of the best wines, the most beautiful scenery, the most delicious cuisine, famous philosophers, artists, and writers. It is the country where people risked their own lives to save three members of my family, including me—people who did what they knew was right. It is also a country where Captain Alfred Dreyfus was falsely accused of treason, and where before and during World War II, many were complicit with the worst evils imaginable: the informers, the police, the bureaucrats, the banks, the industrialists, and the clergy.

Who can say how many of France's people stood on the right side of justice and goodness, and how many stood on the side of evil and debauchery? And who can say without hesitation that they would have done what was right when faced with punishment or death if they did not cooperate or collaborate?

In 1995, on a remembrance day for the roundup at the Velodrome d'Hiver that took place on July 16-17, 1942, France's then-president Jacques Chirac said:

> These dark hours sully our history forever and are an insult to our past and our traditions. Yes, the criminal madness of the occupier was seconded by the French, by the French state—the land of the Enlightenment and of human rights, of welcome and asylum.

It is with mixed emotions that I have returned many times to France to enjoy the treasures of the country, but also to grapple with what happened to me and to my family. I have also returned to give thanks to those brave souls who befriended us, who took care of us, and who made sure that we were saved while risking their own lives.

Visiting Claude Radzinsky in Paris

I had stayed in touch with Claude Radzinsky, my boyhood friend from Marmande whose dear mother and father had given aid to my mother during the war years. She was a wonderful friend and support to my mother. I will be forever grateful for the kindness she extended to my mother, to Herbert, and me. They gave us meals and created a sense of normalcy when we went to their home. They were truly a magnificent family.

In the 1970s, Judy, my children, and I went to Paris and visited Claude. Claude had a beautiful house. He was an engineer, just as he had planned, and held an important job working on the maintenance of the Suez Canal. Over the years, he rose into the upper echelons of French society. He took us to excellent Parisian restaurants and treated us with the utmost graciousness.

The last time I spoke to or saw Claude, he asked, "Can my two sons stay with you for a few months? I want them to learn how to speak English." At the time, we were living in Sherman Oaks in a house that barely had enough rooms to accommodate the family we had, much less two more boys. We had only a master bedroom, a room for my daughter, and a room for my son. It would have been necessary for his two boys to share a room with my son. I thought, *How am I going to do this?* I didn't feel right intruding on my son's space, so I told Claude it wouldn't be possible for his sons to stay with us and that he would have to find other accommodations for his sons.

Claude was extremely annoyed with my answer. Given everything Claude's family had done for my mother during the war and how gracious they were to us when we visited them in Paris, I don't really blame him. After that, he would not speak to me, and he never forgave me for what appeared to be my selfishness. I had fallen short of his expectations of me. Perhaps I should have found a way to house his boys. I lost a good friend.

Évian/Annecy

In the summer of 1997 Judy and I stayed in Annecy, which is near Évian, for three weeks at a French language school so that my wife would have some intensive basic instruction in the language, and so that I could brush up on my French as well. It is a beautiful area referred to as the "Pearl of the French Alps," situated on the banks of Lake Annecy, 35 kilometers south of Geneva, Switzerland. Annecy was awarded the "Golden Flower" in 2015, which is given to the nine most flowered cities in France. The city has a canal flowing through it, and the lake itself has the bluest water in all of France. Cézanne painted the lake many times.

During our stay there, we visited some of the ancient buildings and museums. One weekend, I made the diligent effort to see if I could locate the village where Herb and I had been hidden with other children before we were moved to Lourdes to escape the Nazis, who were on the lookout for Jewish children.

Judy and I went to Évian, and there I located the office of the tourist bureau and asked them to help me identify a village where I was hidden with other Jewish children during the war. I provided them with the geographical points as I remembered them. In their view, the best that they could tell me is that I must be referring to a village on the "Plateau de Gavot," right above Évian. They gave me the names of two or three villages to see if one of them might be the one I was looking for. It was frustrating for me that I could not remember the name of the village, but it wasn't surprising, since I was only eight or nine years old when Herbert and I were sequestered there so many years earlier. And of course, we moved around so much. I couldn't write, and I didn't keep a diary.

We went, looked around, and inquired at a different tourist bureau. Finally, I was directed to an inn that was run by a woman who they thought lived on the Plateau during the war and would have some recollection of Jewish children hidden there. During the winter, the inn was used as a ski lodge. During the summer, it was used as a place for groups of children to stay on vacation.

The owner of the inn showed us a room, and it wasn't familiar to me. She told me that she didn't know where I might have been hidden. She couldn't remember any Jewish children or where they were housed, though she knew that they must have been in the area. She knew that members of the underground had been active in the Maquis, the French Resistance movement during the war. She knew that the Maquis had acted in battles with the Germans, and she knew that Jewish children who had been hidden in the Plateau had been arrested, and many were killed. But she was unsure of the exact location of the village that I was trying to locate. She suggested we come back the next day when her son would be there, who was more familiar with the geography of the region.

Having had this discussion with her, we left the room that she'd shown us and started to exit the hotel to look for a place to spend the night. All of a sudden, a troop of young boys in different forms of dress—some with pajamas, and others still in street wear—came marching through the inn, following one another in a procession. They were obviously staying there for the night.

This was one of the most stunning and dramatic moments of my life. In a flash, this image brought back memories of that period of my childhood. We, too, were like them. We were children just like these children. I was one of them. I saw myself in this line. It was me. That was what I looked like—a young boy following instructions, moving toward a task, whether it was to eat a meal or prepare for bedtime.

I don't think I ever experienced such a vivid moment of recollection in my entire life. It was not like looking in the mirror or looking at photographs of oneself. It was as if I were seeing myself in flesh and blood in a place that was just like the memory I had of that time. I was both the onlooker and the actor. I was looking at myself when I was their age, living under similar conditions, but for highly different reasons. It was very surreal and frightening. One of those boys could have been my younger self—my doppelgänger.

From that moment on, my quest to revisit the places where I spent two and a half years of my childhood intensified. That vision of the young boys walking in line triggered my desire to uncover more of my personal history that I had buried for so many years.

Marmande/Saint-Pardoux-du-Breuil

In 2000, when I was sixty-six years old and at the height of my law career, I contacted the children of Pierre and Jeanne Ros in Saint-Pardoux. Their parents were no longer alive, but most of their seven children were. I best remember Lino, who was my age, Ida, who was a bit younger, Oscar, and Irma. I wanted to make a pilgrimage of gratitude to thank them for saving my mother during the war and to revisit the farm and the village. I arranged a party for them and their family members together with Judy and me, our children, and our four grandchildren. It was important for me to expose my children to what I had been through and to meet the people who treated me *comme les siens*, as if I were part of their family.

I organized a luncheon, and everyone assembled—even a cousin from Paris who made the trip to meet us. Irma, the eldest daughter of Pierre and Jeanne Ros, was the leader of a musical group and played the accordion, which made for a very festive occasion. The restaurant served special black mushrooms from the woods, the kind I ate when I lived in Saint-Pardoux. Tasting them sparked memories for me, like Proust's *petite madeleine*. I used to adore eating them. It was a very loving occasion, although my children and grandchildren felt somewhat out of place. They did not fully understand the importance of this occasion to me.

During the party and at a subsequent visit to Marmande, I learned many facts about my life there and what had happened to my parents during the time that Herbert and I were separated from them. For example, when the police came to the Ros home, they hid my mother in a closet in the Château de Cuq, owned by the Baronesse de Ferrier, where Jeanne and Pierre worked as sharecroppers. The Baroness knew that my mother was hiding there, but she said nothing to the authorities.

During the luncheon, one of the guests spoke with me, and what he told me came as a shock—it was like a bolt of lightning. He said that when my father was taken away by the police and sent to Drancy, they would not allow him to take his prayer book with him. They snatched it out of his hands. Somehow it was retrieved by one of the villagers.

Fragments of his daily prayer book were distributed among the villagers, almost as religious objects to worship and preserve, much as religious Catholics might preserve the bones of saints in reliquaries throughout the world. These fragments were considered holy by those who held on to them. Although they could not understand the prayers because they were in Hebrew, they must have drawn strength from them and hoped that they would somehow bring my father back if they were preserved. Some of the villagers slipped these fragments inside the prayer books they took with them to church.

The guest then gave me a large envelope that contained some of the fragments he had collected to return to me, preserved all these years. I am sure my hands were shaking as I looked at them, touched them. These fragments were part of my father's daily ritual of prayer that he repeated every day of his life until he was taken prisoner by the Nazis. I have them with me to this day. I thanked this villager for giving them to me. They are a way for me to connect to my father and a symbol of his devotion to Judaism. I only wish that they had manifested the faith that these villagers had in these fragments to save my father, but it was not to be. When I close my eyes, I can still see my father davening and whispering the precious prayers that guided him through his days until he was arrested and dragged to Drancy, and from Drancy to Auschwitz, and from Auschwitz to Majdanek.

With the shock of discovering the fate of my father's prayer book still palpable, we left Saint-Pardoux and went to Marmande, which was but a short distance away. We probably followed the same route that our family walked along fifty years ago when we were exiled from Marmande to Saint-Pardoux with only a few belongings and relocated to a barn on the farm. The farmland was still magnificent, but the memories that I carried with me distorted the beauty and brought tears to my eyes, especially when I thought about my mother, so lonely as she sat sewing at her table, making clothes for the local farmers and the blacksmith and wondering where Herbert and I were and whether her beloved husband was still alive.

We visited the Boulevard de Mare in Marmande where my family lived and where my father conducted religious services for the immigrant Jews looking for a place to pray. I am sure that he read from the pages of the siddur, the scraps of which I now carried. (The word "siddur" means "order" and comes from the same root as "seder," the special Passover meal.)

During our visit we had lunch with the secretaire of the city of Marmande. He came from the Basque region of France. I was presented with a bottle of wine, and by the time we had finished lunch I was quite drunk. Then we went to dinner across from his house, but I was still full from lunch and had no appetite. Our host asked, "Why do you come here and you won't eat?" That is truly bad manners—to be invited to a meal and to leave a full plate. I apologized.

Two newspaper journalists from Bordeaux interviewed me during our trip. It was front-page news and included a photograph of Judy and me with the extended Ros family members in Saint-Pardoux. The articles emphasized that we were considered part of their family, and that they thought of us as their flesh and blood, even though we were Jews and they were Catholics. To all of us, it made no difference.

A Pilgrimage to Lourdes

From Marmande we traveled to Lourdes. Prior to our visit there, I had contacted the Archdiocese of Los Angeles and asked for assistance in making contacts with the clergy in Lourdes. Sister of Mercy Mary Jean Meier, the director of the Los Angeles Office of Special Services for Cardinal Mahony, sent letters and emails to France and found out that there were twenty-one congregations of nuns in Lourdes who might have been part of the order that had protected me. When asked why she went out of her way to research this information, she said, "In light of the Jubilee, it was a beautiful year for Mr. Lakritz to be able to say 'thank you' for a gift that was given to him."[22]

---

[22] The Jubilee happens every fifty years, and this Jubilee which took place in 2000 mentions sins against "the people of the covenant." Cardinal Edward Idris Cassidy,

I told Sister Mary that I was angry that Pope Pius XII didn't do anything to help the Jews, and that many Catholics colluded with the Nazis. I pointed out that the teaching of the Church described the Jews as Christ killers. Perhaps I said too much, since she was only trying to help me. She listened to my comments carefully, especially those in which I described how loving and caring the nuns were to me (one of the many paradoxes of my story). She counseled me, "You should never forget, but you should forgive." I have tried to do so, but it is difficult, especially when I am reminded of my father's birthday or the date of his death. On those days I struggle the most.

Armed with this information Sister Mary provided me, I was able to determine that it was the Sœurs de la Charité de Nevers who had sheltered me. Of course, none of the nuns who were there during the war when I lived on the church property were still alive, so I expressed my gratitude to the Mother Superior, Sister Marie-Ange Mesclon, for everything that was done for me—how the nuns hid me from the German military, fed me, clothed me, and showed me love and compassion.

I asked Sister Marie why the nuns did what they did for me. She said that her order "takes care of desperate souls—and the more desperate they are, that's who we take care of." Her response made clear the motivations of those nuns who saved me.[23] I told her of my visit to Catholic authorities in Paris to find out if there were any records of children hidden by the clergy in Lourdes. I wanted to know if Alfred LaCroix was on a list. I discovered that no records were kept because it would have been

president of the Pontifical Council for Promoting Christian Unity, acknowledged the faults committed "against the people of the covenant," the Jews.
[23] From an article in *Tidings*, the Catholic newspaper, January 5, 2001, published by the Archdiocese of Los Angeles, one of the largest archdiocese in the United States.

too dangerous to do so, as it would have proven to the Nazis that the nuns and priests were actively sheltering orphaned children, some of whom were Jewish like me. The Sister knew that this was the case.

When they heard why my family was in Lourdes, some of the nuns eagerly escorted us around the grounds of the basilica, which was under construction for repairs. The gold crown atop the basilica was mostly hidden with scaffolding. It certainly was not the crown as I remembered it; it appeared much smaller to me, and not as sparkling gold. The mountains that we could see behind the basilica also looked substantially smaller in height and size than I remembered as a child.

In the same vein, facing the basilica there is a statue of the Virgin Mary. I remember her very well because I walked by the statue every day while I lived on the grounds; I would sometimes stop and stare at her. Perhaps she had a message for me. She also was much smaller than I remembered. I'm sure that this phenomenon is a common one to adults who return to the places of their youth and are shocked at the changes in the size and dimension of what they recall.

When Judy and I went into the grotto, I described to her how sad and abandoned I felt, how I cried and how I prayed for the safety of my parents. And then I added, "The Sisters saved my life. That is why I needed to come back."

Back to My Birthplace

Unbeknownst to me, during this time several historians were researching the Jewish community of Kiel and uncovering the names of families who perished during the war years, as well as those fortunate individuals who survived. Else and Hans

Molzahn, residents of Kiel and devout Christians, found our family name among historical documents. In a letter dated December 21, 2000, they sent me a map of where my family's compound in Kiel was located, along with other information that they unearthed in their research. In their letter to me they said:

> In order to be able to construct your family tree, certain kinds of lists from the residents' registration office [in Kiel] were instructive. We dug very deep in the cellar of the town hall...in order to give you an idea of what kind of documents we took the puzzle pieces from, we added two of about fifty pages. While doing this research we were getting more and more ashamed because of all the cruelties our German people have done to your family. We again want to express to you how sad we are because of what your family suffered from our people. We hope our results will serve you in making a family tree. We would be glad if you would be so kind as to fill in missing names and figures in our rough copy of a family tree or correct wrong details and then convey them to us.

How many other Jewish families they researched I do not know, but it must have taken them months to gather all the documents related to the Weber-Lakritz family. No lawyer could have done a more thorough job!

The Molzhans suggested to the then-mayor of Kiel, Henning Stademann, that he extend an invitation to Judy and me, my brother, Herbert, and our cousins living in Israel and Australia to take part in a special citywide celebration from June 14–21, 2001. The dates coincided with the city's famous annual regatta, and we were to be the city's guests of honor. A scholar from the University of Flensburg, Dr. Bettina Goldberg, was also conducting her own independent research about the Jews of Kiel. She wrote me a letter asking if I would be willing to meet with her while we were in Kiel so that she might interview me for a scholarly paper. Of course, I agreed. Naturally, there wasn't a lot I could tell her, but I was very interested in what she could tell me about my family. I have her report, which was awkwardly translated into English. The paper was presented at a commemoration of the victims of the Holocaust in Kiel on January 27, 2002.

I had not been to Kiel since escaping with my parents and my brother and fleeing to Antwerp in 1939 after Kristallnacht. I interpreted the invitation from the mayor as an act of repentance for the crimes that were perpetrated against us as part of the small Jewish immigrant community of Kiel. In that spirit, I felt a desire to participate in the various activities planned for us. We were told that all our expenses would be paid for by the city.

Herbert would have nothing to do with this invitation, but I learned that some of my cousins on my mother's side would also be there, which would give us an opportunity to reunite once again. They included Ruth Weidmann, who left Germany for Palestine in 1937, and her son, Max Weidmann. Max served in the British army and the intelligence corps during World War II, and was living in Australia where the invitation reached him.

I did not anticipate that a visit to Kiel under these circumstances would be traumatizing or would reignite bad memories. After all, most of the people now living in Kiel were not the perpetrators of evil or sympathizers of the Nazis. I went to Kiel with an open mind and curiosity about what I would find there.

I'm glad I did. Kiel was delightful. I put aside whatever residual anger I had buried in my heart and enjoyed the hospitality immensely.

Judy and I visited the site of our home and warehouse with the Molzahns. It's not there anymore. It's now a sports arena, which is the biggest money-making venue in the city. Some might say that we deserve a financial piece of that property, but it's a moot point. We cannot get the property back. The German reparations system goes only so far.

I also went to the Jewish Museum in Rendsburg. The exhibits include photographs of children in the Hebrew school that I attended before we fled. In the picture are some of my thirty-one relatives who were killed. A recent visitor to the museum described it this way:

> It is a very moving experience to visit this museum in Rendsburg near Kiel. It is housed in the oldest maintained synagogue and torah school in the northern German state of Schleswig-Holstein and therefore also serves as a historic monument and memorial place. It is unfortunately rare to visit a synagogue building in Germany that survived World War II. The permanent exhibition is about the history of the Jews in Schleswig-Holstein and the Jewish religion. At the time of writing this review there is a temporary exhibition about the Jews who survived World War II and returned to Schleswig-Holstein, most of them until they could get away while a few stayed. The difficulties that they encountered in a society that highly ignored their sufferings and losses are displayed. This temporary exhibition is particularly thought-provoking and moving.[24]

---

[24] Lene R, comment on "Jewish Museum and Synagoguge, Rendsburg," *Klarna.Trips*, July 22, 2020, https://trips.klarna.com/en/adp/germany/rendsburg/jewish-museum-and-synagogue-a7264189605/.

The main event during the week we were in Kiel was the annual regatta, which was splendid. Inaugurated in 1882, the regatta is the largest sailing event in all of Europe and attracts millions of people each year and thousands of competing boats. There is also a *Volkfest* during the week. I was glad to enjoy the Kiel harbor, which I had explored as a little boy. During the war it was hit time and time again by the Allied forces to deter the Germans from deploying bombs and submarines. It was a strategic target because of the German navy base, and the Allies made sure to leave it in ruins by the end of the war. (After the war the Allies participated in the rebuilding of German cities and its economy as a bulwark against Communism.)

Another event during our stay was a formal reception held by the mayor for all the guests of honor, along with city officials and Ellie and Hans Molzahn. The mayor and I spoke extensively at that event. I told him I was happy to be there, even if I was not happy about the reasons why we were there. I was emotionally and mentally torn. He told me he understood. He showed us some photographs of Kiel during the war. One photograph depicts a man walking on piles of snow. In the background is the main cathedral of Kiel, partially destroyed, presumably by Allied bombs. He asserted that the people of Kiel resent the Nazis almost as much as we do. They rightfully blame the Nazis for the destruction of their own city. During World War II, the city was continuously bombed. Eighty percent of the town's buildings were destroyed and 167,000 people were left homeless.

The mayor told me, "I can't explain what happened. The country went crazy." And yet, he also insisted, understandably, that there was a limit to his emotions. "You can't blame all of us," he said. "I had nothing to do with it." I feel in my heart that all

Germans should not be expected to carry the guilt of their forebearers, but I do think that they must acknowledge what happened and find a way to honor those souls who died at the hands of the Nazis. The current generation is sensitive to the ills of the past, and Germany today has the strictest laws against the expression of anti-Semitism of any country in Europe. But there are still those—under the cover of darkness—who harbor hatred against Jews. It is hard to entirely erase the past. There is an expression that applies: "Those who forget the past are condemned to repeat it." Many countries of western and eastern Europe are challenged with the phenomena of neo-Nazi groups who even today adopt the slogans that Hitler espoused to mobilize his followers. Good Germans must be reminded of their past and pay homage to those who died. It is only right.

In Kiel, there was just one small memorial to World War II and to the suffering of its people. There were also what are called stumbling stones, small plaques on the ground with the name of the Jewish person who lived in that building and who was taken away to their death. Since 1995, these stumbling stones have been installed in many cities as a reminder of the past. These almost imperceptible memorials are called *Stolpersteine* in German. Similar stones can be found in other eastern European cities and in Spain and Portugal.

When the mayor invited me to write an entry in his private book of remembrances, I wrote that the city needed a proper monument—something simple but powerful and visible that would commemorate the lives of those Jews who were lost. The mayor watched me write those words, and I know he read them. Whether he and the other officials appreciated what I wrote in very blunt terms, I do not know. As an attorney, I am not one to mince words, and I am sure that I criticized the city for doing so little. I envisioned a tree of life that would hold a prominent place in the city and be visible to all who walked by. Stumbling stones that people could simply step over were not enough.

At some point during our stay, the Molzahns took me to the cemetery where my sister, Rosa, is buried. She is the only member of my family who has a burial plot. All of my thirty-one relatives who were led to slaughter are ash and bone scattered somewhere in Germany, Poland, or elsewhere in eastern Europe.

I never heard back from the mayor about my suggestion for a prominent and visible memorial. However, about ten years later, in 2011 or 2012, I received a copy of Kiel's major newspaper. A front-page article with photographs discussed the dedication of a monument. It was exactly the monument I had asked for. The monument included a large plaque, a cement pole, and behind it a living tree in commemoration of *all* the Jews who died during the war. It is located in a plaza not far from Kuhberg Strasse where my family's compound was, and where the city's main sports arena is now located, in plain view. Amazingly, my Israeli cousins were there for the dedication—and I wasn't invited or even informed!

I don't know why the city waited so long, and I don't know why they didn't invite me. Maybe they were afraid I would come and shame them. Or perhaps they felt insulted by what I had written in the visitors' book. No one ever mentioned it to me, but I felt by not being invited they were sending a strong message to me that I was not welcome. Or perhaps my invitation was lost. I will never know. Be that as it may, at least my family members and other Jews who perished are properly acknowledged.

222 | Alfred J. Lakritz

Addressing Oakland Tech

Throughout the three years that Herb and I attended Oakland Tech, we did not share our personal history of the war years with our classmates. We wanted to blend in, to be just like all our friends. They knew that we had come to the United States from France but that was the extent of what they knew, and they knew this only because of our accents, which we tried to erase. But in 2003 I was contacted by the Oakland Tech Alumni Association to write a letter as part of an effort to gather the memories of former students, and I chose to do so. I am sure that what I wrote came as a surprise, however I wrote it not to shock anyone but rather to thank the students and the school for what they did to help Herbert and me. The first part of the letter summarizes our childhood, while the second part addresses the Oakland Tech community:

> Our lives were saved by the courageous and giving Jews and Christians [in France]. All of them, including nuns and priests, have our greatest regard and gratitude for their kindness and humanity in the face of certain arrest if they were discovered.... [O]ur father, along with the hundreds of thousands who were also condemned, died a horrible death....

> The three years at Tech allowed us the entry into a normal stream of life in this society. Herb and I share a great debt of gratitude to the administration, teachers, counselors, and all the wonderful friends that we made at Tech.

> I will never run out of ways to say "thank you."

Testimony Given to the U.S. Holocaust Memorial Museum

I became very active in the Heritage Lodge of B'nai B'rith in the San Fernando Valley. I ran for office and won several times over the years, and as a representative I had many important exchanges with Rabbi Harold Schulweis, who moved from San Francisco and had a pulpit at Valley Beth Shalom in Encino, California, near where my family lived. He was a great spiritual advisor to me and a real inspiration on many accounts.

I sometimes shared my wartime experiences with members of the Lodge. Many members were not familiar with the stories of children who were hidden by the nuns and priests and were moved around France by the OSE, being trailed by the Nazis and members of the German military. On one occasion, one of my fellow Lodge members, and perhaps also Rabbi Schulweis, encouraged me to give testimony to the United States Holocaust Memorial Museum, which was interested in recording the many stories of survivors, mainly those living in the United States. After some reflection, I felt it was my duty to bear witness and share my experiences to shed light on what had been done directly my brother, my parents and me. In 2008 I went to Washington, D.C., and was interviewed for five hours by a member of the staff, Gail Schwartz. She was extremely impressed with my memory and my sharp attention to detail. I assured her that everything I told her was true, that I had the facts to back up what I was saying, that I had done extensive research of my own about my family.[25]

I am glad that I gave oral testimony to the United States Holocaust Memorial Museum. But those recordings are only a small part of my story.

[25] My testimony is available online, and those of my readers who wish to hear a somewhat younger Al Lakritz (I was then 68) can access what I said here: https://collections.ushmm.org/search/catalog/irn35973.

Epilogue

There are hundreds, if not thousands of memoirs written by survivors of the Holocaust, each one different because of the personal details, experiences, and emotions that the writer shares. I now add my words to this library of memories with the intention of bearing witness to what happened. I wish to crush the efforts of those individuals who would deny that the Holocaust happened or claim that the number of those who died were far less than what was reported. My lost relatives were thirty-one among six million.

For years after the end of World War II, many survivors remained silent, but with the publication of some of the books I have cited in this memoir, the floodgates of truth have been opened. There are now archives around the world preserving these books and memories, including the United States Holocaust Memorial Museum in Washington, D.C., the Shoah Foundation at the University of Southern California, the Mémorial de la Shoah on Rue Geoffroy l'Asnier in France, and Yad Vashem in Israel.

Contributing to the awareness of the Holocaust are numerous films, most notably *Schindler's List*, directed and produced by

Steven Spielberg; *Life Is Beautiful,* directed by and starring Roberto Benigni; *The Garden of the Finzi-Continis* directed by Vittorio De Sica; and *The Boy in the Striped Pyjamas,* directed by Mark Herman, as well as documentaries *The Children of Chabannes* by Lisa Gossels and Dean Wetherell; *Weapons of the Spirit* by Pierre Sauvage; and the nine-hour *Shoah,* produced and directed by Claude Lanzmann, to name a few. (I mention these books, documentaries, and films for my readers who may wish to learn more about the Holocaust.) Each one contributes a piece of the puzzle that attempts to answer the question: how could this have happened?

I hope that my memoir helps in some small measure to address that question as well, to address that the mystery of human beings is their capacity for good and for evil. My plight was caused by the eruption of evil on a massive scale. It was amplified by sympathizers, opportunists, and many people who, understandably, simply wanted to save themselves and stay out of the Nazis' way. And yet, there were so many heroes. My brother and I are alive because of people who maintained their goodness—who saw the Nazis for who they were and, whether Christian or Jewish, French or German, civilian or soldier, did what they could to feed, clothe, shelter, and protect two little boys. I think about how many other good people did the same for so many others in need. They were loving, generous, and ethical. Those people defeated the Nazis just as much as did the brave Allied soldiers who fought them on the battlefield. There were two wars going on at the same time that intersected—the war of the Axis nations to crush their neighbors and dominate the world, and the war of the Nazis to eradicate the Jews. Between these two wars was chaos and destruction.

I hope and pray that this memoir honors the memory of my beloved father, Simche Weber, and my mother, Marjem Weber, as well as the members of my family who were not fortunate to have been saved.

What I did not get to say to the consul general who had asked me about traveling to France, because he was pulled away by other guests, is:

"I owe my life to the righteous people of France who, in spite of all the dangers that surrounded them, chose to help my mother, my brother, and me. To them I say a heartfelt *merci mille fois*—thank you one thousand times."

* * *

I have written this memoir as proof that the Holocaust was real and that evil did take place, but there were also righteous people who risked their lives to save innocent people like me. I want to convey that I am an ordinary man who suffered extraordinary losses at the hand of evil, for no sin other than the accident of my birth. I have lived a life that I have earned in order to prove that those who saved me did so with some reward, whether they asked for it or not. Whatever mitzvahs I have performed in my life—whether working as an arbitrator or mediator without pay, winning a lawsuit so that justice prevailed—are all acts of gratitude from the man who was born Alfred Weber and is now known as Alfred Lakritz. I have also labored over these pages in order to pay tribute to a righteous and honorable man, my father, Simche Weber, and his wife, my mother, Marjem, who was an angel placed on this earth to protect and nurture me.

To both of them I owe my life.

I end with a stanza from a poem by W.H. Auden called "The Musee des Beaux Arts," which describes accurately and absolutely the state of suffering:

> About suffering they were never wrong,
> The old Masters: how well they understood
> Its human position: how it takes place
> While someone else is eating or opening a
> window or just walking dully along.

Article in *le Republican*, September 22, 2000 in which Judy and I visit with members of the Ros family, in Saint-Pardoux-de-Breuil. The caption says: "Alfred Lakritz and his wife among their friends who they consider family." I am 66 years old when we made this return trip.

Article in the *Mas-Agenais* with a photo of Judy and me with the Ros family. The headline reads, "A voyage of memory."

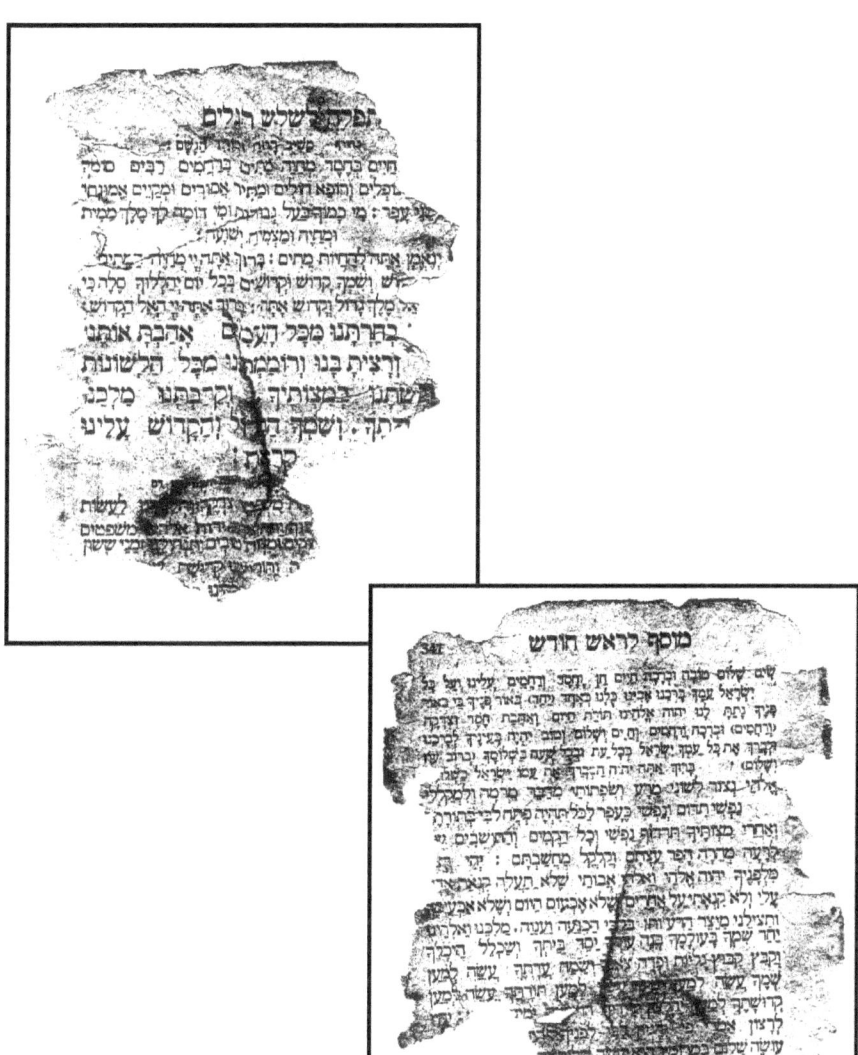

Fragments of my father's prayerbook (siddur) that were distributed among the
villagers of Saint-Pardoux-de-Breuil after my father, Simche Lakritz, was arrested and
taken away to Drancy and from there to Auschwitz and then to Majdanek.

At Lourdes saying thank you to Sister Marie-Ange Mesclon, Mother
Superior of the Order of the Sisters of Nevers.

In Kiel, during the famous boat regatta where we were guests of the city.
(L-R) Norbert Gansel, Mayor of Kiel, city official, Judy, me,
and another official, June 2001.

Flotilla of boats during the Regatta.

At the port of Kiel during the celebrations. (L-R) City official, my cousin Max Wiedmann, who attended the festivities with us, unidentified individuals; Judy and me.

Signing the mayor's guest book, June 2001.

Acknowledgments

The Holocaust has been remembered in thousands of books: fictional accounts, histories; and memoirs. This is my attempt to add to the library that exists in the belief that each survivor has a unique perspective on what happened and why.

I spent many years gathering documents that helped me piece together the tragedy that befell my immediate family – my mother, my father, my brother, and me.

As a lawyer, I didn't want to write a book that could not be backed up by facts, by proof, and that is one of the reasons that it has taken me so long to write *Adieu*. The other reason is that I didn't have someone to help guide me along in my effort, to encourage me to keep going when the facts became so overwhelmingly tragic that it was more than I could bear.

Three years ago, Matt Friedman, the Associate Regional Director of the Anti-Defamation League, introduced me to Loren Stephens, president of Write Wisdom, and an ADL National Commissioner. She and Josh Stephens spent several hours with me at our home in Calabasas and I easily made the decision that I wished them to help me write this memoir as I was unable to finish it on my own. The memories were too painful. They spent many hours interviewing me and then collaborated on six drafts and a final manuscript which we agreed to title, Adieu, after the words on my father's postcard before he was dragged off to Gurs, Drancy, Auschwitz, and met his ultimate horrific death at Majdanek.

Many people contributed directly or indirectly to the writing of this book and to the collection of documents. Else and Hans Molzahn, residents of Kiel, Germany, my birthplace and the former home of some of my family, searched maps and archival documents to establish that we had lived in Kiel. They shared with us drawings showing where my grandfather's property was located. In 2001, the Molzahns made sure that we were invited to a special celebration in Kiel, and took me to the gravesite of my sister, Rosa. To Professor Bettina Goldberg of Universitat Flensburg, Germany, who interviewed me for a history paper while I was in Kiel I owe many thanks. I am also indebted to Marie Juliette Vielcazat-Petitcol, author of *Lot-et-Garonne: Land of Exile, Land of Asylum*; and my translator, Sylvia Brandon-Perez; for providing an indepth analysis of my temporary home in France, and the politics of the region where I spent a number of years in hiding with my brother, separated from my parents, who had turned us over into the hands of strangers in order to protect us.

I am also indebted to Gail Schwartz, a member of the staff of the U.S. Holocaust Memorial Museum, in Washington, D.C., who interviewed me for five hours on tape in 2008. She gave me a very special compliment observing that I had an excellent memory for names and places. When you live through something horrific, the smallest detail can leave a lasting impression.

In discussing the scope of this book with Loren and Josh, it became obvious that I needed to also share the good fortune I had in starting a new life with my brother and my mother after we were allotted visas to the United States. After the war ended all I could think of was coming to America, but that dream would not be realized for five long years.

I would never have believed when I was a teenager hiding in the Basilica in Lourdes with the nuns and the priests, that I would one day graduate from high school in Oakland, California, attend the University of California at Berkeley, earn a law degree at one of this country's most prestigious institutions, marry Judy Lenoff, and have a happy family life and a fulfilling legal career. So many generous souls in America helped to make all of that possible including the Fasses, Rabbi Harold Schulweis; and the many teachers and volunteers at Oakland Tech. And a special thanks to Stan Gold, who advised me about the law and guided my mother when she considered divorcing her second husband.

I had the opportunity to return to Germany and France with my adventurous wife to explore the cobblestone streets, the vineyards, and the farms and to reunite with some of the extraordinary people who sheltered my brother and me. I cannot remember all their names but I want to cite in particular the Ros family, Henry Berney, Gerard Guillot and the Radzinsky family, most especially Claude, as well as the Sœurs de la Charité de Nevers at Lourdes, who with or without directives from their liturgical superiors in Paris and Rome made the decision to give me a safe haven. I also wish to thank the OSE and HIAS who at various times saw to my safety and safe passage to the United States.

It is my fervent prayer that *Adieu* will sway those who believe that the Holocaust never happened, or that just a few lives were lost instead of the millions who perished at the hands of a monster and his minions.

And I further pray that my story is proof that good can triumph over evil when virtuous people stand up and do what is right.

www.ingramcontent.com/pod-product-compliance
Lightning Source LLC
Chambersburg PA
CBHW071153130626
46553CB00004B/1640